Hot CX
Customer Experience
For Realists

Gary Moss & Andrew Stothert

BRAND VISTA | Customer Experience Alignment

Brand Vista
Brunel House, 3rd Floor,
56 Princess Street,
Manchester,
M1 6HS,
Website: brand-vista.com

Every possible effort has been made to ensure that the information contained in this book is accurate at the time of going to press, and the publisher and authors cannot accept responsibility for any errors or omissions, however caused. No responsibility for loss or damage occasioned to any person acting, or refraining from action, as a result of the material in this publication can be accepted by the editor, the publisher of either the authors.

ISBN: 978-1-5272-1759-1

Typeset in 11/14pt Garamond and in 12pt Calibri Light.

FOREWORD

Nick Varney, CEO Merlin Entertainments

It was 1990 when I began a love affair with the attractions industry that has so far lasted my entire working life. I had just arrived as Marketing Director of Alton Towers theme park, fresh from an early career in fast-moving consumer goods where I had been marketing famous brands such as KitKat, Quality Street and (less sexily) Harpic. I was immediately beguiled by Alton Towers, with its majestic gardens and quirky, eccentric atmosphere. We often said that it possessed a real magic in contrast with Disney's fantasy magic. But there was something missing: the magic wasn't quite getting through to the customers. Part of this was the pressing need for new investment, which was soon delivered. However, the rest was to do with the people who worked there and their attitudes, which were partly summed up by the 20 per cent responding to a staff survey that 'Alton Towers would be a great place to work if it wasn't for the visitors'. Clearly, there was a disconnect between brand promise and delivery.

The ensuing journey in which Andrew and Gary (later founders of Brand Vista) became closely involved was one in which the true meaning of brand alignment was discovered. Every element of the brand promise was dissected and built upon using extensive research amongst our customers and staff (stakeholders, in the modern parlance). Ultimately, a brand promise and delivery framework was put in place, ranging from compelling advertising through to a brand-driven customer experience. At the heart of this was the insight that was to become a Brand Vista trademark: the distillation of all the functional and emotional values into a single, defining brand essence. In Alton Towers' case this is defined today as 'fantastical escapism', and it is the litmus test on which all new attractions, communications and, importantly, staff training is assessed. Today, Alton Towers Resort enjoys Net Promoter Scores in the excellent range and has one of the biggest Facebook fan groups of any UK consumer brand.

In this book, the Alton Towers story and numerous others are used to demonstrate Brand Vista's unique approach to customer experience and brand alignment, and in particular the overarching importance of this feeding through into the teams that are ultimately responsible for delivery. It goes without saying that this is of preeminent importance for brands in service industries, but in my view, any company serious about brands and long-term business models ignores it at their peril. Many other agencies and consultancies have since piled into the new, 'undiscovered country' of brand alignment, but as the authors note in their introduction, they discovered it first and therefore have a longer, richer story to tell.

CONTENTS

ACKNOWLEDGEMENTS

We couldn't have written this book without the help of many, many people.

Our first thank you is to Nick Varney. He has no idea how much an influence and inspiration he has been to us over the years so we owe him more than a few beers and probably some royalties (though he has no chance of the latter). But he is far from the only person who has contributed.

We feel enormously privileged and fortunate to have worked with some brilliant people who have placed their trust in us and let us into their companies to do our stuff and, by and large, made it fun. A huge thanks to all of them, too numerous to mention by name.

We have also worked with some people who have driven us nuts! They've caused us to put our heads in our hands and yell to the skies. We'd like to thank you too. The challenges you presented us with have enriched the experience and helped us learn how things can go wrong.

And of course, all our Brand Vista colleagues. They have brought ingenuity, excitement and challenge to everything we do so that we can never stand still; they simply wouldn't let us, it's the only way to keep CX 'hot'.

And, finally, thank you for reading. We are sure you will not agree with everything we have said, of course you won't. who are we trying to kid? But, we are humbled that you have given us your time; we hope you enjoy it and find something you can apply in the real world.

INTRODUCTION:
TAKING THE PLUNGE

Coming out was a massive moment in our lives.

We had been ad men, brought up on the belief that advertising could achieve anything. We came out in 2000 as customer experience evangelists who believed that customer experience is the present and the future and was probably the past as well, only we were not allowed to say so. It was a big thing to do at the tail end of the last century, but we could deny it no longer: the old model was dead and the new one was so much more real and exciting.

This book is about one of the most dramatic business transformations in history. A pivotal change where customer experience (CX) became the battleground for business. We have been involved in this battle from day one; in fact we were probably fighting the early skirmishes well before we even realised we were in it. So our book is written by realists, not bothered by industry awards or recognition. It's more a 'how to' book based on what we know works – and doesn't – for you to share and debate. It's as simple as that. So if you want lots of academic analysis and theories written in business speak, this book is not for you. This is a punk version of CX, based on the experiences of people who are not shy about their mistakes and are quite happy to share their secrets.

October 2000

We had just resigned our senior jobs at J Walter Thompson and the powers that be wanted to know what we were going to do next. What was so compelling that we were giving up our nice little earners and handing back our company car keys? Suspicion reigned, and the firm had some very expensive lawyers circling. The truth is, we'd have loved to tell them – we knew exactly what it was, but we had no idea what to call it.

We had been brought up in the white heat of retailing and, more pertinently, the visionary world of leisure marketing. Our big moment was winning a pitch in 1991 to work on the repositioning and rescue of Alton Towers with the then marketing director Nick Varney, now CEO of Merlin Entertainments. This changed our lives as we quickly became immersed in the development of the Alton Towers customer experience.

From day one, it was fantastic! We were involved with elements of branding that were normally outside the remit of advertising agencies. We helped align processes, new product development, the culture, recruitment and training, as well as communications, to a simple vision for the brand. Our work with Nick and his team convinced us that the Mad Men days were over and we were no longer 'in advertising', and although we didn't know what to call it at the time, we were customer experience (CX) professionals and we needed to 'come out'.

So it was 'bye, bye, JWT' and the world of advertising. This all seemed very exciting at the time, but there wasn't a 'new world' to replace it – we were making it up as we went along. We wanted a revolution, the emergence of a whole new customer experience sector, and yet it didn't exist. For us, in 2000, it felt quite lonely.

How different the world is now. The revolution has finally come.

A 2015 Gartner survey discovered that 89% of companies expected to compete mostly on the basis of customer experience by 2016, compared to 36% four years previously.

By 2020, customer experience will overtake price and product as the key brand differentiator.
(2013, Walker)

Every week, there are customer experience conferences in different parts of the world, and for every sector you can imagine. There are numerous courses and workshops, and people are levering 'customer experience' into their job titles whenever they can. Some practitioners have become 'rock stars of CX' and cannot cope with either the demand for their expertise or the requests for their mere presence at conferences and gatherings. Customer experience has become a profession in its own right and now embraces both the physical and digital channels of delivery, and making it compelling has become the number-one obsession for businesses and organisations globally.

"In the old world, you devoted 30% of your time to building great service and 70% of your time shouting about it. In the new world, that inverts." - JEFF BEZOS – CEO, Amazon

CX improvement is the hot topic for business because, quite simply, it can be transformational: it can accelerate the progress of what is already successful or rescue something that is failing. As these figures show, customers reward 'Hot CX' with loyalty and publicity, so it is easy to see why companies rush headlong into achieving it.

- 68% of people tell others about 'brilliant customer experiences'
- 48% will not buy from a brand if they find out that a friend has had a bad experience
- 58% of people give a company only one chance to get it right

(Research conducted by Brand Vista, 2016, using a nationally representative sample)

But CX improvement is not enough.

Merely improving the customer experience does not necessarily make it compelling, irresistible or, dare we say, 'hot'. It does not maximise opportunities and could leave you vulnerable. The efficiency and satisfaction gains delivered by CX improvement are highly prized and difficult to achieve, but as more and more companies 'improve' their CX, the more homogenous they become; what is seen as differentiating one month becomes standard practice the next.

This book goes beyond 'improvement' and outlines a different approach. It is based on the premise that, in order to remain compelling, drive differentiation, maintain customer focus, inspire colleagues and ensure success,

4

companies need to use their brand to drive CX development. This means aligning the brand's positioning, values and personality to what the business needs to achieve and hard-wiring it through the CX where it matters most. We call it 'Hot CX'

"A brand is a living entity, and it is enriched or undermined cumulatively over time, the product of a thousand small gestures."
MICHAEL EISNER, CEO, Disney, 1984–2005

We have been arguing the merits of using the brand to drive success since we left JWT in 2000, but very few people, if any, have been saying the same thing. In the first years we called this approach 'brand alignment', but because the term 'brand' often gets mistaken for design, distanced from the business imperatives and put into a bucket marked 'fluffy creativity', it gets ignored and overlooked.

This has baffled us for years, and is all the more puzzling when putting the brand at the centre of CX development delivers the difference, focus and unifying inspiration that everyone craves. Branding has not gone away – in fact, it has never been more important – but the method and skills that you need to 'brand' have changed dramatically. It's now done through the customer experience.

There is so much evidence to show that this approach works that it is difficult to know what to leave out, but here are a few facts and figures to be getting on with. Greater alignment brings 12% higher customer loyalty, 16% higher profitability, 18% higher productivity, 25% less staff turnover in high-turnover companies and 49% less in low-turnover companies, 37% less absenteeism (Gallup, 2010).

Looking further for evidence, we point to the real-world success of some of the companies who practise 'Hot CX', such as Merlin Entertainments, which in 2013 floated on the London Stock Exchange with a valuation of almost £3.4bn; Shop Direct, which, over a period of two years, saved nearly 100,000 hours back to the business; or The Jockey Club, which has enjoyed eight consecutive years of turnover growth and reversed long-term attendance decline. Hot CX has also formed the sales stories of many venture-capital-backed companies and underpinned the transformation of numerous established organisations by reigniting their teams and making their proposition compelling.

You will want to know where all this 'experience' comes from. In the early days, we were lucky enough to learn by working with brands such as Madame Tussauds, Chessington World of Adventures Resort, Warwick Castle, Sea Life, Silverstone, Barratt Homes, Hertz, Compass Group, The Jockey Club, The London Eye, Tui Group, The Science Museum, Gala Bingo and Coral. We worked with retailers such as Hamleys and Total, towns like Blackpool and cities such as Liverpool. We also worked with business-to-business clients that you may never have heard of, such as Brookson, OAG and BLM. We had some fantastic successes, some crazy failures, a whole lot of fun and every day we learned something new about how to make customer experience work in the real world.

We did all this between 2000 and 2007. Nobody had heard of us (you probably still haven't). JWT had forgotten all about us and the lawyers had stood down. We appointed a PR agency, which sacked us because they felt we didn't want publicity. And they were right. We were still learning and didn't want to make fools of ourselves, and we were determined to find the right way to make CX compelling and differentiating so that we could be confident it worked. So we carried on learning and, since 2007, have continued to work with our great friends at Merlin across all its brands. We have also added others, such as David Lloyd, AstraZeneca, Asda, Stonegate, Vision Express, Betfred, Enterprise Inns, Mitchells & Butlers, The Times, Hotter Shoes, Police Mutual, Sit-Up Ltd, Spirit Group, Russell Hobbs, Cosatto, Prezzo, Odeon, the Harry Potter franchise and a very famous bank that we are not allowed to name.

The more experience we gained – both good and bad – the more we learnt what it meant to 'use the brand to drive compelling CX'. Without question, Hot CX is omnichannel – or 'channel neutral', if you like. Whether the channel is physical or digital, it's all the same; it's customer experience. We're not the ones saying that, customers are. They simply don't care about the channel. For them, it's all one company, brand or organisation that they have chosen to deal with, whether that's by phone, online or in store. When we talk about CX in this book, that is what we mean: Hot CX is the experience in its entirety, across all channels.

Hot CX is silo bustin', data rich, fast and flexible. It drives revenue and cuts costs. Hot CX forces differentiation, keeps customers central and colleagues inspired. Hot CX embraces the dreamers and the realists of this world, it reaches for the stars while keeping its feet firmly on the ground. It works by aligning the customer and employee experience, the business needs and the vision for the brand. It has to do all these things – anything else just isn't hot.

Hot CX does not mean producing the greatest, most mind-blowing customer experience that wins endless awards. It means using the brand to drive a compelling omnichannel customer experience that drives business successes. That last bit is the key in this context, as Hot CX is not an end in its own right; it has to drive the success that you have targeted at the start, however you decide to measure it.

Financial failure is definitely not hot.

We have divided the book into five sections, but that's not to say this is an end-to-end linear process that cannot be changed depending on the starting place or any short-term needs. Flexibility and adaptability are key in this regard, and the journey can be taken in chunks, with moves backwards and forwards as necessary. So although these five stages may present the purest version of Hot CX, in the real world, going from one to five in a linear fashion rarely happens.

Section 1 is called Exploring. You will probably have heard the expression, 'A house must be built on solid foundations if it is to last'. But you may not have heard the rest of the saying: '...otherwise you will sink back in to the soft ground and be swallowed up by the world of illusion'. Exploring is the critical foundation stage of developing Hot CX. It outlines the need for immersion in the wider business and its objectives, how to investigate and interrogate the attitudes and behaviours of customers and colleagues in ways that get to the truth so that your foundations are strong and real. It argues the need for inspiring research that looks at things in different ways, providing new angles, and how it all needs to be backed up with data.

Section 2 is called Visioning. It describes and uses examples to show how to develop a vision for your brand that acts as the driving force for your omnichannel CX. It outlines how the vision can act as a filter through which the business, at all levels, decides what it does and doesn't do and how it should be done on a daily basis. Visioning covers the importance of creating the vision in alignment with the objectives of the business, its capabilities and resources. It describes how and why it should be created collaboratively, with input from every level, how it can fail and how wonderfully transformational it can be.

Section 3 – Aligning. This is the stage that makes this approach different. In fact, if someone else has already provided great insight and created a compelling brand vision that you all believe in and think is right for the business, you can skip the first two stages and jump straight to Aligning. This is where we take the vision and turn it into a compelling omnichannel CX. In this section, we present evidence that shows why Aligning will deliver the sustainable business difference of the future. We tackle the CX versus UX debate and give good and bad examples of alignment, and we share practical ways in which to achieve it in the real world. We introduce 'brand basics' and 'brand amplifiers' and look at ways to create them using exciting, new, innovation methods. If you read only one section of this book, make it this one.

Section 4. This is the Delivering section, where we list the assets you need to implement CX properly and turn your plan into action. We talk about the importance of getting the right people involved, keeping your feet on the ground but never losing sight of the vision, and how to build a blueprint for delivery that your teams will buy into, feel inspired by and compelled to deliver. We make sure that the whole process does not feel daunting by stressing the importance of piloting and prioritisation. We also cover ways that the process can fail. In short, this section is a practical guide to making sure that all the Exploring, Visioning and Aligning actually lead to a new, possibly transformational CX.

Section 5 covers Measuring and how to make sure that you measure the right things at the right time. It divides the metrics you need into two types, lists them and ventures that current techniques are outdated and one-dimensional before giving a solution that embraces one metric that the professions use most in a new and easy-to-use way. This section is evangelical about how measuring – rather than being a dry, 'must-do' element of Hot CX – is actually its catalyst; a bringer together of people, a buster of silos and a driver of progress.

Section 6 is titled 'Hot CX for B2B'. We thought that, rather than jump from B2C to B2B throughout the narrative, we would simply look at B2B on its own and point out where the differences lie. The truth, though, is that there is very little difference. We all have customer experiences, whether we are operating in a B2B or B2C environment, or even a charity, a customer-service provider, a town or city or government department. We are all delivering experiences, and the principles are 95% the same.

Throughout the book we will stress the importance of using every-day, non-gobbledygook language, engagement and hard-nosed planning. We will cover the use of existing process-improvement techniques and adapting them for Hot CX development, of going with the grain of a business to minimise disruption, using specialist skills where they are needed and saving money at every opportunity. 'Frugality' may be too strong a word for it, but a form of it is central to Hot CX. We will also list top tips in an easy-to-reference format and end each section with a summary of 'what is hot' and 'what is not', so you can cheat and get the basics of 'Hot CX, Customer Experience for Realists' very, very quickly.

Back in 2000, we didn't know any of this. We set off down the road in the dark without a torch. We have learnt the hard way and have been through a sort of transformation ourselves, from traditional ad men to passionate CX professionals. This meant we had to get real – and boy, have we done that! We know that customer experience development has to be rooted in the ambition that the business has, and that the board and the frontline teams need to be involved or you are wasting your time. We learnt that if you don't back things up with numbers, you are simply sticking a finger in the air, and if you try to be too clever with words and theories, you will be laughed at. We also know that you can't hang around pontificating, trying to get things perfect, because 'perfect' doesn't exist. Realism is needed to succeed in the long run, and 'improvement' is not enough to be compelling, so you have to use your brand to make your CX your own and deliver success.

In 2000, when we started out, we wrote a slide – it was probably our first and was almost certainly not a slide at all but an acetate.

> *The first era of branding was that a brand is what it says it is.*
> *The second era of branding is a brand is what it does.*
> *We are in the era of experience branding.*

Then, in 2015, we went to a conference and saw our slide from 2000. This one had the exact same words as ours, but this time delivered by KPMG in its keynote address as 'new news'. Pah! So we have been galvanised to start turning up the volume and share the realism of brand-driven CX delivery before we forget it all. And 'share' is the operative word, as our whole journey has been one of sharing; it's what life is all about, and we have been lucky enough to share with some wonderfully talented and generous people who let us and our teams into their companies to do what we do.

We hope you enjoy Hot CX and find it useful. We also hope that, at its end, you'll feel compelled to engage with us and discuss the topics we raise, because we are still learning and will probably never stop, so we would love to hear about you, your experiences and what you think, especially about the future. One thing is certain, though: coming out was the best thing we ever did, and we're glad we took the plunge.

1. EXPLORING

"If you do not know where you come from, then you don't know where you are, and if you don't know where you are, then you don't know where you're going. And if you don't know where you're going, you're probably going wrong."

TERRY PRATCHETT, I Shall Wear Midnight

We said in the introduction that this approach to CX development is different to others. We also believe it is more effective and sustainable. Its standout difference is that it puts the brand centre-stage (more of that later, in Visioning), but one of its other differences is its direct and thorough alignment to the business needs and commitment to the brutal truths of customers', consumers' and colleagues' attitudes and behaviours.

It's a fact: you can't set off on a journey unless you know where you are starting from and where you want to go. The Exploring stage makes sure that you set out on your journey with the odds stacked on your side. This means knowing exactly what the business is trying to achieve and over what timescale, what resources are available, where you stand with customers, consumers and colleagues and what future options are possible and most rewarding. We have found that the more comprehensive, brutally honest and inspiring the Exploring stage is, the hotter the eventual CX will be. Without it, you could set off in the wrong direction, get lost and end up in the wilderness.

Setting off from a place you know

We have come across many businesses willing to set off on their CX journey in the pitch dark. They feel their way, using hunches, instinct and hearsay. They either don't believe what their customers or colleagues tell them, or are reluctant to spend a few thousand pounds on what could be a multi-million pound journey. Either way, they think they know best and set off. Sometimes they are right, but mostly they get it wrong. Gut feel has its place in business, but more often than not, these people will misread their customers or overestimate how good their company actually is.

80% of CEOs believe their customer experience is great. Only 8% of customers agree. (Bain & Company, 2015)

Most companies prefer not to work in the dark. Instead, they establish their starting place and work out the options for their route and final destination. They make sure that the Exploring they do gets to the truth, is inspiring, forward-thinking and robust. The Realist also ensures that the company keeps its ambitions realistic, as they know there are always restrictions on budget, time, competition, the ambition for the business and its customers. Companies that don't explore in this way should not set off on the journey – they should stay put, not move a muscle, stay in the dark.

Since our formation in 2000, we have tried every form of Exploring imaginable. Some of it has worked and some of it, painfully and regretfully, has not. For the creation of this book, we have trawled through the different types of Exploring – across all channels we have used that we know are necessary to successfully set out on the journey towards Hot CX. We have divided these into three types, each driven by a different basic objective. Fortunately, and conveniently, they all begin with the letter 'I', so we are calling it 'The Three Eyes of Exploring'.

The Three Eyes of Exploring

1.   IMMERSION
It is key to know what the board's issues and needs are and what the customer-facing teams think about the process and brand they work with and the customers they serve.

View from the top

Your Exploring should always start internally and at the top of the business. The leadership team knows the short- and long-term business ambition and the strategy to get there, and can monitor progress across the whole business. In short, the team sees the big picture and knows how it will evolve in the future.

Immersion at the top will help identify the:
- Short-term business imperatives
- Medium- and long-term ambitions for the business
- Time frame for delivery
- Corporate attitude to customers
- Capability to change
- Existing sources of customer research and data (nobody wants to reinvent the wheel)
- People who need to be involved
- People who are against any change (they need to be embraced and convinced)
- Barriers to change in the past
- Resources available, in time and money, to make it happen
- It should also establish technology platforms, technical constraints, data flow and management

View from the front

Frontline colleagues know what is and isn't working with customers. They see the opportunities and problems that the numbers don't reveal, and they usually know why things are the way they are. However, it is amazing how infrequently these vital frontline teams are heard.

The brutal truth is that these are the people who – day in, day out – deal with customers online, over the phone and face to face. They know what gets in the way of a potentially friction-free customer experience and what poor and good CX looks like. The Realist knows this and taps the resource.

The frontline team unlocks secrets about the brand's relationship with its customer, their needs, motivations and their view of the current CX. They are brilliant and brutal at identifying problems before the business numbers reveal any issues, and they are a rich source of practical ideas that, outside of CX development, would often have no natural outlet. The Realist also knows that when it comes to implementing changes, the change is more likely to stick and succeed if people on the frontline have been meaningfully involved and feel part of the project.

So, when developing the CX, *always* involve the frontline team at every stage, and, if you can, do so first. They will save you a lot of time, tell you where to look and apply a healthy dose of realism to everything thereafter. It is also worth going there yourself: listen to calls in the contact centre, spend a day on site, jump on a truck and make deliveries or answer complaints. It doesn't take long to get a view from the frontline, and you will never regret it. We love it and think other people do, too.

Working with a well-known bar brand, we ran groups with bar staff, door minders and head-office administrators. They told us the brutal truths about the standing of the brand, the obstacles to improvement, and gave us some brilliant ideas on improving matters. They also completely changed the board's view about who was actually coming into their bars: the board had previously thought it was 'sophisticated professionals', but the team knew it was really 'up-for-a-laugh office workers'.

Working for an insurance company, we spent time in the contact centre, interviewing call handlers and listening to service calls. This helped us segment the audience, identify issues for further investigation, and it gave us some clues as to our next steps.

A large national retailer was convinced that show-rooming (when people use their mobile phones in store to compare the price of goods online) was becoming more and more of a problem for them. We spoke to staff on the shop floor, who dismissed this: 'They're just playing games and wasting time on Facebook like everybody else.' The bosses were unconvinced, so we carried out intensive testing with large samples and ingenious mobile phone tracking techniques. It turned out the people on the shop floor were right all along. The bosses could have saved a lot of money by listening to them.

For one global retailer, we were asked to find out why many of the board's initiatives that focused on up-selling to customers were not having any effect. We looked at internal staff surveys, which revealed that 80% of staff were either very satisfied or satisfied working for the company, but some quick analysis of the open-ended questions told a very different story – one of disconnection and frustration.

So we ran a series of internal workshops and found a number of brutal truths, including this gem.

In an environment where the front-of-house staff were earning minimum wage, the frontline team were made to arrive half an hour early to put out newspapers before their shift and stay half an hour afterwards to cash up. As one team member put it to the board: 'Why on earth would I want to sell another Mars bar if you take an hour a day from me?'

Despite the obvious additional cost, the company found a way to change this and the transformation was electric, with future up-selling campaigns breaking all targets. The level of staff turnover declined significantly, all of which was predicted by the business case put together by the team. This had a big impact on profitability and provided the context for future CX changes.

Way back in the 1990s, in our JWT days, we were carrying out some competitor research on Marks & Spencer. Our monitoring revealed a slip in its delivery scores based on staff feedback. Six months later, M&S's sales collapsed, followed a few months later by the share price.

This was not really a surprise, as we backed these quantitative measures with our own mystery shopping and found a disconnected and uninspired front-of-house team who, for the first time to our knowledge, were bad-mouthing this once-great company.

So the front of house knew before the management or The City. Of course they did.

Engage through asking

We started this section talking about a journey towards Hot CX. Your frontline teams, the board and don't forget your suppliers (never forget your suppliers!) are going to be with you on that journey and need to believe in what you are doing if you are going to succeed. There is a body of evidence suggesting that engagement leads to business success.

Engagement through the brand has operational and financial benefits

- Companies with high and sustainable levels of engagement throughout the brand had an average operating margin three times higher than those with lower engagement levels

- Organisations with engagement levels of 65% or more had shareholder return 22% above the average. Those with engagement levels of 45% or less had shareholder return of 28% below the average

(Sources: Towers Watson 2012, Aon Hewitt 2011)

'Engagement' is an overused phrase, but it is key to the development of Hot CX. It applies throughout the business, especially in the boardroom. It has been proven time and time again that it is better to get the views of the senior team out in the open as early as possible. The Realist also knows that the personal hopes and dreams of people must be considered. If you are to succeed, ignore the personal side at your peril. People want a legacy; they want association with success and their contribution acknowledged. The Realist makes this happen.

2. INVESTIGATION

Consumers and customers must be central to the new CX, so they need to be central to its development. That may seem like a statement of the bleeding obvious, but many customers tell us that the CX they encounter has been developed for the company by the company and they feel that, at best, they are a last-minute consideration. This happens all the time. It probably happens to you when you are using websites and apps, trying to navigate a telephone service system or working your way through government bureaucracy. We can almost hear your cries of anguish, your 'aargh!', your expletives, the throwing of phones and shouting at computers. We can see your blood pressure rising, the pulling of hair and oh, how we can hear you losing all control when confronted with a sales assistant who has just asked you to go through 'what went wrong' for the 15th time while your parking meter ticks away and your daughter desperately needs a wee. We know all this and we sympathise. We have been there countless times and we will probably be there again – most likely at some point today.

Something is wrong. Many companies are either not doing it right, have raised unfulfillable expectations or simply do not care. They will tell you verbatim that 'understanding the attitudes and behaviours of consumers will be key to their success'. Unlock the truth of what consumers think and why they do what they do and your version of Hot CX will also be theirs. Fail to understand, and you can wave goodbye to Hot CX and say hello to irate consumers and lost market share to those who do.

Finding the truth in the hard and soft stuff
Investigating is understanding what your customers and consumers do and don't do, and how they think. To get an accurate, robust and truthful picture that guides the direction of your omnichannel CX requires a combination of data derived from the business and your digital platforms (hard data) and market research (soft data). One of the beauties of digital data is that it can show a truth that is untainted by opinion, and this approach can be applied to other environments, too.

Wherever you are starting from, you will need to raid your digital platforms for data, go back to customer-research reports, knock on the financial director's door and get access to sales and operational data. There will almost certainly be the need for new analysis of existing data and the commissioning of new market research to find out the things you do not know. While this may seem onerous, time consuming and costly, it doesn't necessarily need to be, especially if you have the attitude that '90% right is acceptable', respect the limitations and strengths of the different forms of data and are prepared to roll your sleeves up, accept help and make a few informed guesses. It all leads to one thing – understanding, and if greater understanding leads to a more compelling CX, then it also leads to competitive advantage.

The aim of the investigation stage is to establish how customers, consumers and colleagues use the brand and the customer experience as it is and what they think of it, how this compares with the competition and what it could be like in the future. It needs to identify how the brand makes and loses money, where it is losing it and where the opportunities to make more lie. It must also identify the basic elements of delivery of the category and where there is opportunity to amplify the brand and differentiate.

A drop of the hard stuff
Take an omnichannel view of the numbers. It never ceases to amaze us how often opinion masquerades as fact when it comes to customers and their relationship with brands. This is a bit odd, as there is usually a mass of rich data available across the business that can help prove or disprove hunches, identify issues and highlight opportunities across the whole CX.

The best approach requires a crashing together of the CX–UX debate and taking an omnichannel view. As we have been saying all along, digital- or people-based interactions are all one CX to the customer, regardless of channel. This makes it necessary to get a team together from across the business who can represent every touch point in the CX so decisions can be made about what data is required and how you are going to use it.

The most compelling business cases for CX development are usually when business and market-research data are combined to build the case. It's a fact.

Data exploration will tell you when people are dropping out of your CX, whether that is digitally or physically. It will also tell you when they are happy, satisfied and predisposed to recommendation and buying more. Equally, it will tell you when they are annoyed, dissatisfied and motivated enough to complain and tell the world. It will tell you where the holes are and where to dig deeper. There will be things you can't figure out from data alone – and you will need to investigate these further – but, essentially, data analysis provides the proof and gives companies the confidence to take action.

Experience audit
In the investigation stage, we are establishing the start point. The numbers are key, but the analysis is often done in a haphazard way. It needs structure.

Wherever the hard data comes from – be it financial, sales, digital or customer service – it can be looked at under the following headings. This provides rigour and makes it more usable:

1. Achievement: how well customers achieve what they want to achieve in your omnichannel customer experience. It requires an understanding of what specific 'jobs' they are trying to complete at each stage and how successful they have been at completing them..

2. Find Out: how well customers can get the information they need to interact with you. This could be as simple as looking up the opening times of a retail outlet, finding out the things they need in order to book a hotel or go to a concert, or getting social services support.

3. Life Fit: more often than not, the CX needs to fit into people's lives so they don't have to break the stride of their daily routines. This could be anything from looking up train times to buying sandwiches.

4. Satisfaction: engaging with companies should be a positive thing and meet the expectations your brand sets. In some instances, this will be a smile on the face; in others, it will be the satisfaction of simply getting what they want, whenever they want it, wherever they are. Satisfaction is a measure of the degree of overall satisfaction and enjoyment that people have with the CX.

5. Pick Up: interactions with brands can last a while. The ability to put down an interaction and then pick it up later on a different device – whether by phone, online or in store – is a key indicator of satisfaction.

6. Transfer: the way that the data flows around a company can reveal a lot. If, for example, digital data is held in silos, it means that basic customer expectations of personalisation can be impossible, or queries and complaints cannot be treated seamlessly and be friction free.

The Experience Audit is a structure to analyse the masses of data circulating, sometimes aimlessly, around a company. The focus can then be applied wherever there is greater need, goals can be set against the various elements, benchmarks with competitors identified and correlations can be established with the main KPIs of the business as a whole. The audit should cover both the physical and digital channels – or, in other words, it should be truly omnichannel.

At this point, it is worth mentioning that working out what is going on is not magic. It requires analytical skills, some of which are specialist. The analysis will give you the hard facts that are needed to take action to satisfy consumers, who are often unreasonable and demanding, feel empowered enough to take on big corporations and can easily take their custom elsewhere.

Proving it with numbers is where the CX Realist wins over the CX Dreamer every time. The robust data and analysis gives visibility to the board about where transformation is needed and where priorities for the business lie. It enables comprehensive business cases for transformation to be developed at an early stage, which normally means that there is commitment and that any change required will be given the resources to make it happen.

It's all in the numbers

We worked with one of the big mobile telephone operators to improve its omnichannel experience. Our main focus was improving the path to purchase, but when we delved into the data on the company's website, we realised that a huge number of help queries were ending suddenly halfway through the journey. We posited that failed help queries online would turn into expensive-to-serve enquiries to the call centre. Subsequent changes to the website saved £1.5m annually in call-centre costs.

A touch of the soft stuff

A drop of the hard stuff is not enough to provide the understanding that is needed to develop a truly compelling customer experience. Data analysis provides measurement, but it cannot give you total understanding without exploring the emotional part of the equation and establishing the 'why' behind the 'what'. Therefore, you need to look at the hard data alongside what is often called 'soft data' to find out what customers really, really want.

Interrogation's what you need

Interrogation doesn't have to be nasty, but it is necessary. To get an accurate picture of the here and now, and where the brand-driven CX can go, you need to get real, get to the truth, use psychology and get inside the heads of the people who matter.

Some of the techniques we describe here are applicable at whatever stage you are at, or whoever you are talking to. You can't simply ask questions without at least a little bit of interrogation and expect to get the brutal truths and business-changing insights you need. The CX Realist knows that people tell lies, they like to show off, they forget stuff and they have selective memories. People are also all very different. Some think in pictures, some like numbers, some are very expressive and some are 'deep' and like to keep their views to themselves. It's like a game, and we use techniques that get to the truth, get into the psyche and acknowledge the fact that, just because people are quiet or have a limited vocabulary, that does not mean that they don't have anything useful to say.

Here are some hot interrogation techniques you can use very easily.

Collage – 'say it with pictures'

We live in a visual world and we all know that a picture can paint a thousand words; using pictures to generate a story about a brand, therefore, helps people express their feelings in a much richer way. Also, many people find it difficult to express themselves in words and need props or stimulus to help them articulate what they really mean.

We tried using clay in a similar way. The results were amusing but useless. Don't even think about it.

Pictures can be the catalyst

We were researching the brand standing and CX of a global oil supplier in Cornwall and were looking for clues on how to position it, how to identify the brand of delivery and the emotional connection that we thought customers might have. In one particularly memorable group, we had an extremely quiet man who said nothing for 75 minutes. He only looked at his feet and seemed completely uninterested in discussing the brand and how important the service it provided was – that of delivering oil to his house. We then asked the team to tell us what the brand and the product meant to them in pictures. The man gathered his cut-out collage, sat down and returned to looking at his feet before it came to his turn.

When it did, we all turned to him, wondering what he was going to say.

Using the pictures, he told of his utter dependency on the oil company, how it was the lifeblood of his household, and that if it let him down, he felt personally responsible and that he had not fulfilled his 'man-of-the-household duties'. The collage was the catalyst for him to reveal his innermost self and emotions. His delivery was extraordinary and we will never forget him.

We asked some customers of a global retailer to rate the company out of 10 for the quality of its CX. The scores averaged 7.4 – not great, but also not too bad, according to our client. We then asked customers to show us what they thought of the CX in a collage, and this is an example of the comments they came back with. The explanation was equally revealing: 'the service is angry', 'they don't want us there', 'they can be aggressive'. So, that's what 7.4 really means – it was a shock to all concerned.

Seeing is believing

We wish we could reveal the client on this example, but it wouldn't be fair. Let's just say it is a national health-related retailer.

We ran focus groups with customers, with the objective of establishing the potential direction for the brand and to isolate where we could amplify the CX. After discussing the sector and the brands in it, we took customers shopping and, when they got back, asked them to create a collage of the ideal shop in this sector.

Until then, our client was convinced that a certain part of the experience was central to the offer; the element on which they should focus everything about their brand and CX.

Not one person included this element in their collage.

The potential amplifier the client had in mind was nothing of the sort – it was a basic to consumers, not even worthy of mention in the ideal shop. Of course, if we had come back and simply relayed the information to the senior team, they may have ignored us, but the collages were brutally revealing. This client is now the leader in its highly competitive high-street market place.

Treemen – 'using child psychology'
The treemen has a big success rate, also known as blob tree.

When you want to know how engaging your CX is, use treemen. Depending on your outlook, it is stolen, or borrowed, from the world of child psychology and was developed to help children tell their teachers how they feel about the big relationships they have in their lives. Of course, children do not have the vocabulary or the articulation of an adult and may struggle to express their true feelings. Treemen unlock all this and the truth comes gushing out.

Used in the context of brands and CX, it helps people articulate how they feel about complex brand relationships in a simple and effective way. They select one or more treemen that they believe capture their relationship with the brand.

The example on the next page shows how it works.

The person is responding to the question, 'How do you feel about your relationship with X?' (A well-known financial brand.) As you can see from the treemen the respondent selected, it reveals that the respondent feels unhappy, lost and unwanted, but there are times when the company gets it right and truly understands the respondent's needs. It is with further interrogation that you can find out why this is the case, isolate the pinch points and have the potential to fundamentally change the course of a business. If we had simply asked the question, 'How do you feel about x?', we would probably have received a bland response that was no use to anyone, including the respondent.

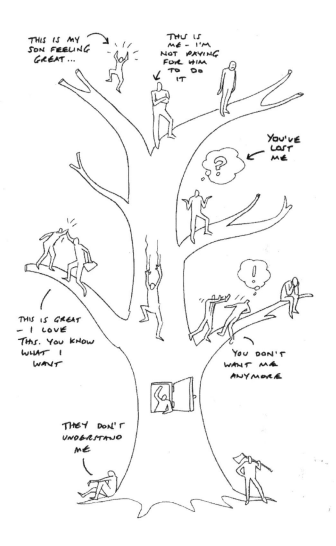

On the pull?

We used treemen to get inside the heads of twentysomething nightclub customers and what they liked and disliked about the clubbing CX. We decided that we needed to go 'to the jungle' for this job and set up in a pub next to the club on a Friday night. A professional recruiter selected people who were queuing for the club and brought them to a room where we used the treemen technique. Remember, it is 21:30 on a Friday night: this had the potential to be very entertaining and a little bit dangerous.

The treemen did their work, though. Some of the young men circled the lone treeman sitting on the end of the branch as their big fear. They used this treeman to express their fear of being 'left behind' while their mates had 'pulled'. Others circled the axe treeman to illustrate their fear of the intimidating bouncers. None of this would have come out in a traditional focus group, and we concluded that if this technique can get to the truth in this environment, it can do it anywhere.

Create conflict for natural debate
This is a great technique for forcing debate and getting to the truth.

It works by running two groups who have different views or different behaviours. To be effective, these groups must initially be run separately and then brought together for the conflict element.

Often, putting them together is like lighting a blue touch paper.

The technique works by allowing one set of people to explain, justify and argue why they think or do something with a group of people who think or do the opposite. These then become natural discussions, and although the obvious challenges arise, the truth will come out. When the sessions work well, the moderator has little to do.

Biker rage

We once got two sets of bikers into a conflict situation – what could possibly go wrong?

We were exploring an insurance brand's multi-channel CX and its positioning and were trying to isolate what, within the CX, was key and what values were perceived by the different types of bikers.

One group insured their bikes through the 100% Real Biker insurance company (the company was definitely not called that, but let's go with that for now) and paid more for doing so. The other group bought their insurance through a household-name insurance company and paid less – but, of course, the household-name insurance provider is not a 'real biker' brand.

The Real Bikers were asked to explain why they were prepared to pay more. After a fairly rational debate about the CX, the emotion began to emerge, a few insults flew and it became extremely heated (remember, we are talking about insurance here), and we knew we were getting to what really mattered.

As a result, we were able to reassess the entire CX, the tone of voice and the way the brand had to engage its clients to maintain its premium.

We recruited two groups of people who all lived within 20 miles of an historical attraction. One group had never visited, whereas the others were regulars.

After separate sessions, the groups were brought together and we asked the visitors to 'sell' the historical attraction to the non-visitors. The debate that raged told us which elements of the CX were known about, as well as what elements were most appealing and therefore deserving of resources. It proved to be a real eye opener for us all.

This is certainly not an exhaustive list of interrogation techniques; they are just a few examples for the CX Realist, who has to dig deep and find out what people really think so they can work out how to improve the CX, what really matters and where the brand can go. These techniques work just as well with colleagues as they do with customers, and they are worth their weight in gold.

3.   INSPIRATION

The Realist knows that setting an inspiring vision of where the brand could go and what the CX could be like is key. They also know that it can get caught up in the 'here and now' or be too far from reality to make any practical sense. One of the reasons this can happen is that research and analysis is also stuck and does not inspire the change and leap to the future that many of us are looking for.

The inspiration stage of exploring provides an early sight of the future. It is an exploration of the options and possibilities across both the physical and digital side of the CX. It needs to start from what the customers want to do and achieve over a specific timeframe and how the CX can evolve to align to it. It needs to answer questions such as what will the consumer, business and technological landscapes be like? What will people need, want and desire, and how might we be able to deliver it in an omnichannel world?

This research takes a few risks, but without it, the vision for the brand and the aligned CX will be stuck in the here and now and a massive opportunity missed. Boots on, let's 'go to the jungle'.

Jungle research

Keeping ahead of the pack and maintaining differentiation is a common goal, but it is difficult to achieve without taking some risks with your exploring programme. If you want to create an experience that's truly compelling, future-proofed and differentiating, then you need to add a different angle to the programme and do some exploring that nobody else is doing. Without it, the opportunity to create Hot CX will be lost. So, as part of your exploring programme, leave the research zoo of normative research for a while and go to the 'jungle' to experience your brand in its natural habitat and get some different perspectives.

Jungle research involves getting the views of people not involved in the brand or the category but those who have a view about the future. For example, you can talk to psychologists, who can be brilliant for digging below the surface of customers' reactions and adding scientific understanding and evidence to your insights, as well as sociologists, technologists, media commentators, politicians, early adopters and trend setters. You will not find this kind of stuff in the textbooks – but that's the point: it needs to be different, risky and hot.

Jungle research also involves observing the brand in its natural habitat as people are actually using it. Of course, it could be argued that 'jungle research' in this context is merely a different term for more impressive-sounding names such as ethnology or anthropology, but whatever you call it, this kind of exploring takes on board the fact that animals operate very differently in a zoo than they do in the wild. Anyway, jungle research is more Hot CX than any '...ology'.

Jungle evidence

Working with an international holiday company, we wanted to find out what was compelling about being 'outdoors' so that we could set out a new vision for the brand and integrate a new tone of voice. We went to the 'jungle', where we found and talked to a round-the-world yachtsman, mountaineers and trekkers to understand the real meaning of the extreme outdoors.

To understand the fears and worries of cigarette and booze smugglers in order to help plan a different sort of 'customer experience' for HMRC – one that would put people off doing it – we went to the place where it would be easiest to get a group of them together for a chat: prison. Yup, it was scary, but we got great insight and made changes to the CX (for want of a better term) that had real impact.

When we wanted to know where the key touchpoints were for a distribution company, we became a parcel for the day. We found out that to do their job properly and to the satisfaction of customers, many drivers had to break every part of the process designed by head office. This resulted in wholesale change to the CX.

Recently, we have been studying how children around the world learn through play in order to support a client creating a whole new way for its staff to interact with customers. To do this, we spoke to child psychologists, teachers and children.

For a pram manufacturer, we worked with an amazing psychologist to gain deeper insights in to the pressures, concerns and fears of first-time mums and dads so the company could build a more supportive and empathetic customer experience at this amazing but often scary time of parents' lives.

The CX for theme-park brands is key to their success. From the moment people engage online when they research their trip through to their journey home, customers are looking for some degree of escapism, and theme parks need to develop their omnichannel CX accordingly. With the objective of setting out the CX of the future, we got inspiration from early adopters of technology and leisure experiences all over the world, futurologists at gaming companies, social commentators, psychologists and even the government. The output has been a key source of guidance ever since.

The discovery day

The Exploring stage will involve people from a number of different parts of the company. Some will be using digital-data analysis techniques or advanced statistical methods, others will have conducted focus groups, interviewed people one to one or simply observed. There will be a lot of data from different sources and in different formats, and it's inevitable that those who have been exploring will have begun to form opinions and generate ideas. The last thing anybody wants is four or five separate, unrelated reports that lack direction and do not consolidate the situation.

The analysis needs to pull everyone together for a Discovery session. These sessions can often last more than a day and are central to the process overall, as all the evidence needs to be shared and debated before an accurate understanding of the 'as is' situation can be established and, more importantly, new insights are uncovered that point to opportunities for the future. This is done by capturing the pieces of evidence (clearly sourced) on Post-it notes and clustering and connecting them to form the findings of the research. The output then becomes a pivotal document in the process of driving the CX, as it effectively represents the voice of the consumer and the business in the whole process.

The CX Realist uses all three 'eyes'

The CX Realist will do what is necessary to get the business onside, to get inside consumers' heads and hearts and see the real future possibilities. They will also know that it takes more than one explorative technique to do it successfully across the three exploring objectives of immersion, investigation and inspiration.

In 25 years, our exploring has taken us down many a garden path, which has sometimes led to the undergrowth, but we have also scaled the uplands and been to places that other explorers never reach (that's probably enough 'journey' metaphors). The point is we have seen first-hand what does and doesn't work, what provides real insight and what is simply a box-ticking exercise. We have trialled techniques that bombed spectacularly and others that have been unbelievably engaging and changed views by 360 degrees.

You can try to get away without doing one of the other stages, but if you do, you can't be a true CX Realist. By missing a stage, you run the risk of losing the support of the business, running out of resources and energy, being at odds with your customer and consumer and being blind to change and opportunity. No Realist wants to risk that and no CX that is constructed this way can ever be truly 'hot'.

The Exploring output

Your next step is to use the insight from Exploring as an 'as is' starting point for both your brand and customer experience. It represents the first steps on your journey and, if your exploration has been done well, you will be heading in the right direction and it will be possible to show the top team that not only can you improve the customer experience, but you can do it at a cost and effort advantage to the business. Bingo!

When mapping the 'as is' CX for the first time, keep it high level. If you descend into the detail too quickly, you will get bogged down and overwhelmed. Identify the pain points and opportunities for improvement and their impact on the business and map the people, process and technology constraints associated with them.

It may be a statement of the blindingly obvious, but you must focus on mapping a customer journey from the perspective of your customers. Simple to say, but you will be surprised by how quickly teams can fall back into the detail and internalise the work.

Keep the view from the top

This happened with a very complex CX we were mapping with a globally recognised information-based brand. A skeletal customer journey had been mapped in advance, and all the people responsible for the various stages were invited to the session. They all accepted the invite, but only turned up for the 45 minutes or so that we looked at their stage of the journey. They were not interested in what happened in the whole journey, or even the stages immediately preceding or following their own stage. 'Nuff said.

You can plot the journey in a number of ways. Rather than do it using internalised stages, we prefer to approach it through customers' eyes and by the jobs that they need to do at each stage. We need to capture how they feel, what works well and what hurts.

CX mapping can change lives

While mapping the existing CX for a world-famous media brand, a conversation between the editorial and CX teams highlighted the fact that the CX team had access to data that would help the editorial team with a challenge they faced and didn't think they could overcome. It was a revelatory moment!

At one of the biggest housing associations in the UK, the mapping of three different customer-segment journeys at once enabled the cross-fertilisation of learning throughout the entire organisation, especially within one niche area. This helped improve the omnichannel CX for thousands of people.

Keep Exploring

The Exploring stage has three main elements: immersion, investigation and inspiration. If you carry out all three stages by taking a view from the frontline, engaging the company from top to bottom, going to the research jungle to uncover new and inspiring insight, making sure that you interrogate to get at the truth and then prove everything with a drop of the hard stuff and a touch of the soft stuff, you are on the way to Hot CX.

It would be easy to say that is it; your exploration is done; relax. But of course, it is never finished. The moment you stop looking, listening and learning is the moment you start the slow but relentless slide downhill to a place where you have lost connection with your team, customers and consumers in general.

So let's end this section acknowledging the fact that exploring is a continual journey and rejoicing in the fact that if the business has explored successfully, it is now in a position to start looking to the future. The leadership and frontline teams have been engaged and have contributed, your customers and consumers are central to everything, you have mixed insightful, visionary thinking with a healthy dose of realism and everything has been proven as much as possible. What a start to your journey! You are going in the right direction. Or, to paraphrase Mr. Pratchett: 'You will leave for your journey knowing where you come from and where you are, so that you can work out where you are going so that you do not go wrong.'

Thank you again to Terry Pratchett, who kicked off this chapter. You are a CX guru.

Exploring: what's hot and what's not

Hot	Not
Setting off from a place you know	Setting off in the dark with no light
Getting the leadership and frontline involved and engaged	Disappearing into your own silo
Taking an omnichannel approach	Being too channel-specific
Carrying out a structured omnichannel experience audit	Being subjective and judgemental
Using hard and soft data to understand the 'why' and the 'what'	Doing only one or the other

Interrogating to get to the truth	Just asking questions
Going to the 'jungle' for new insight	Doing the same exploring as everyone else
Reaching outside the sector	Keeping it too close
Delivering a consolidated 'as is' view of the brand and the omnichannel CX	Being unconnected and non-directional
Linking insight to business benefit	Insight for insight's sake
Providing a view of what the future looks like	Staying in the here and now
Constant exploring	Thinking it's all over

2. VISIONING

"Never look down to test the ground before taking your next step; only
he who keeps his eyes fixed on the far horizon
will find the right road."
DAG HAMMARSKJÖLD

As you can imagine, we have done a lot of reading over the past few years – blogs, articles, the Harvard Business Review, newspapers and magazines are never far from our desks or screens. We have an insatiable appetite, partly driven by our own values of 'always on' and 'never complacent'. We can't switch off. We have also been to many conferences, spoken at some and even hosted one as a rather strange double act in Brussels. We trawl websites, meet anyone professing to be an expert, read case studies and dive into any new book that does the rounds. We have read the narratives of many 'successful' case studies and analysed data, from the biggest companies in the world to small, niche players that have disrupted their markets. Yet, despite all this information, stimulus and paranoia that we may have missed something, we have yet to find an approach that puts the brand centre stage.

This is what makes this approach different and is the essential ingredient to making your CX 'hot'.

An approach that hot wires the positioning, values and personality of the brand through the CX, at the touchpoints where it matters, ensuring that customers' needs and desires remain central yet balanced with the needs of the business, is more engaging, inspiring, future-proof and differentiating. It is the approach we take and one that works more effectively than any other we know. Of course, we always make improvements when we discover a need, quickly and efficiently using tried-and-tested techniques, but we always do so with the brand in mind.

This means that the creation of a vision for the brand in terms of its positioning, values and personality is a pivotal stage in the creation of Hot CX. It makes up only about 1% of the work involved overall, but it sets the direction and guide for the CX that is eventually developed. This also reinforces just how important the Exploring stage is. In Exploring, we have found out where we are starting from, obtained a few options for the future and started to engage and enthuse people across the business. The vision for the brand will provide the framework for the CX, the guide for new product development and resource allocation, recruitment, service style and many other areas, so if Exploring has been minimal or you have skirted around the big or contentious issues, you are starting from a dangerous place. If, on the other hand, you have done it well, the odds are stacked in your favour, the vision will be the catalyst for success and you will never look back.

Getting the right vision and making it work

A clearly articulated, robustly researched brand vision can transform a business. It can harness the enthusiasm and passion of the people who work there, it can focus effort on what needs to be done, and can save money by providing a lens through which you can decide what should not be done. But many companies get it wrong. They see it as a creative exercise and involve designers and copywriters, when it should be a hard-nosed business decision. The result is often pseudo-intellectual twaddle that achieves nothing but looks awfully clever. Realists never want to go there. It hurts.

Part of the role of the brand vision is that it guides resource allocation. This is important. If you know what you stand for and what your values are, you have a ready-made lens through which you can look at your omnichannel CX and prioritise activities and resources.

A major household-name client of ours applied this vision to its CX and gave itself back 99,082 hours and saved £728, 221, while at the same time boosting revenue by £2.9m in two years. That's Hot CX!

Saving money is not often associated with Visioning, but if change is done through its lens, it will always remain customer-focused and the impact on sales and the brand will, if done well, be positive.

The vision should look forward and be compelling to customers and consumers and inspiring to colleagues. It should set out what the positioning should be, what values should guide it and what personality it should have. That's all you need to create a vision; nothing more – just those three parts. Some call the vision in its entirety the 'compelling brand proposition', and we really like this and have seen it work, but, for simplicity, we will concentrate on these three parts in this section and keep the terminology as basic as possible.

The terminology is often a major barrier to success, though. Those of you familiar with the way advertising and design agencies create visions for the brands they work with may be wondering why we don't have our own trademarkable way of creating a vision. Where is our 'brand onion', 'brand footprint' or 'brand key'? Well, the answer is simple: as any CX Realist will know, they don't work in the real world.

OK, that may be a little harsh, but in a world where CX is king, more people than just the creatives, designers and marketers have to understand it and act on it. Onions, footprints and keys just don't cut the mustard because they use flouncy terminology, which leaves it open to ridicule, ignored or simply misunderstood. None of these outcomes are good for the CX Realist. So bin the fancy made-up language – the vision needs to have one interpretation, and that can happen only by using simple, every-day, directional language. That is the CX Realist's way.

As a guide, we used to say, 'If the burger seller doesn't get it, then we haven't got anything,' but on realising that this is patronising to burger sellers and, quite honestly, the understanding can be equally misaligned in the boardroom, we simply say 'keep it simple'.

'…what really drives [employees] isn't usually money – it's the knowledge that what they're doing matters, inspired by a shared vision, and working towards a common goal. Customers "feel this" when it's present, and love it. You cannot fake it.' (Source: mcorp.cx)

We once asked the board of a national retailer to write down in simple English what their brand stood for. It was early days for us, and we wanted to test how well the vision we had created was understood. We thought the vision that used some clever, made-up English and well-crafted paradoxes with double meanings (OK, I exaggerate to prove a point) was pretty good. I went around the room and only one person had written anything down. His card said 'trust'.

Lesson learned. Back to the drawing board. We'd overcomplicated things and would never do so again.

So, unless there is an established terminology that is understood by all, it is always best to go old school and think: what is the compelling positioning in the market that we want to occupy? What values should drive what we do and don't do? And what personality should we have to guide the way we communicate and deliver our whole CX? That's CX for Realists, right there. Each element must have a purpose, as there is no point having an element to your vision that doesn't guide your brand in a meaningful way.

Here is a way of thinking about it that we use in some of our sessions.

Newspapers have the same raw material to work with every day. Yesterday's news.

Yet the brands in the market all have a different positioning, are underpinned by different values and adopt different personalities. You can all guess what their likely stance will be on an issue, what their view will be, how they will tell the story and the tone of voice and language they will use.

The Times: Sir Fred exposed as injunction breached
Daily Mail: Sir Fred's Affair: Why We Do Have A Right To Know
The Sun: Fred The Bed! Ex-RBS chief had affair with employee

OK, The Sun's headline may seem a bit obvious, but it illustrates the point. The Times tackles the issue of Sir Fred Goodwin's alleged affair by taking a neutral, factual position expressed in a similar way. The Daily Mail takes what could be described as a judgmental, righteous, middle-England approach, demonstrating very clearly where it stands on the issue. And The Sun is, well, The Sun.

And that's the point.

How to maximise the effectiveness of values

Values are powerful, deeply set and should be pretty much immovable. They can also be an immensely powerful part of a brand's armoury. They can be compelling for legions of customers and can drive differentiation. At one client of ours, we have seen a single value drive cultural change and a 25% increase in turnover in a year, but they can be confusing and are often muddled up with personality traits.

We sometimes explain them by describing our business's founders

On the surface, they are very, very different. One has supper, the other has tea. One loves rugby and sailing, and one adores football and feels a bit iffy even on the calmest of seas. One knows his wines, and one just drinks it when the beer has run out. The tea-eating, footballing, beer-drinking landlubber is Gary. The supper-eating, sailing rugger bugger is Andrew.

So why has this relationship survived and thrived for more than 25 years? Of course, regardless of our different upbringings and interests, we share the same values.

Different personality, same underpinning values.

Most businesses do not maximise the potential of values

Our clients are always asking how best to use them. Should we have organisational values (i.e., values that determine the way we work and that are usually developed by HR or Operations) or brand values (the values that customers buy into, usually developed by Marketing), or both?

It is an important question, because without a clear answer there can, at best, be utter confusion and, at worst, complete inertia.

People become confused about what a value is and how it should be used (especially in a brand context). Very simply, a brand value should drive the brand to behave in a way that reflects an aspect of its point of difference. If all the right Exploring and brand development has been completed, consumers will recognise these behaviours and find them compelling.

All relatively simple, but people sometimes think personality traits are values, while some think that organisational values are brand values, and vice versa. In some cases, the brand values are so bland that they are completely useless, and I'm afraid to say that we have lost count of the number of times we've seen 'integrity', 'excellence' and 'teamwork' excitedly unveiled as the new differentiating values. Whether it is confusion or blandness, the result is the same thing: a massive opportunity lost.

So, what is the answer?

Let's face a brutal truth. Making two sets of values work (brand and organisational) is simply not feasible – unless, perhaps, you are an FMCG brand and your team has very little interaction with customers. In this case you can relax for now – but don't be complacent, as the times they are a changin' and many FMCG offerings are becoming more experiential.

For the rest of us, there are two routes to success

Route one. The ideal and purest way is to have one set of values that are differentiating and written with a bit of zing and fizz that makes them live. Primarily, they should be compelling to customers and also guide the way the organisation works. At Brand Vista we practise what we preach, and we have five that operate this way: Happenability, Fairness, Confident Never Complacent and, my favourites, Always On and Vive la Différence. They guide the way we work together but are driven by what we hope makes us compelling. Doing it this way ensures total alignment, avoids confusion and works on the ground.

Still, life is never ideal, and it certainly isn't pure. The 'one set, consumer-driven' route is not always possible in the real world.

Route two. If any of the three criteria below apply to you, you will probably need to do something different:

1. Your immediate business needs dictate that dramatic cultural change is required. A set of values for the way in which the organisation works is essential and urgent. In this case, be bold and make sure the organisational values reflect the culture that allows you to serve your market brilliantly. This demands extra effort from trotting out the standard 'teamwork, honesty, openness' etc, but will have a much greater effect.

2. You may have already embedded a set of very effective organisational values. Changing them or adding brand values will confuse and could undermine them.

3.   You are a 'house of brands'. Your teams move across different brands in your portfolio and you want one set of organisational values that drive the corporate culture.

In these situations, it might be time to consider not having brand values at all. Of course, this route is riddled with danger. If we have only organisational values, we risk becoming bland, especially if the new battleground is 'branding through experience'. We will surely lose if we don't hard-wire what our brand stands for throughout the whole customer experience? It is imperative to keep our brand central, and so the answer is breathtakingly simple: call them something else.

In truth, all that is needed is a clear head and a pragmatic attitude. We have many clients who have worked through the values conundrum and can show the benefits. The best ensure that the brand runs throughout their whole customer experience, even if they call brand values something else. The bottom line is that it doesn't matter what you call them, as long as they inspire and excite and give a clear direction to everyone in the business. They can play their part in delivering the promise of the brand through the omnichannel CX.

So, the brutal truth about making values work is to keep it simple. Have one set, or make sure you know why you have two and don't call them the same thing. The other brutal truth is that experiential branding is the future and getting this right will dictate your success.

To help illustrate how important values are and how the different ones stand out, I once asked a conference of 300 people to write down the three values that drive their lives. This caused a lot of angst as people thought intensely about the answer.

This was the first point. They are important and very deep.

Then I asked the person furthest away from me to read out their three values. They came back with something like 'honesty', 'hard work' and 'teamwork'. I thanked them and then asked the next person to read out their three, but they were not allowed to read out any that had been used before. I went along the line, and the fourth person had no values that had not been mentioned already. The point, of course, is that brands need to have 'stand-out' values that differentiate, as well as 'foundation' values such as safety and cleanliness.

Our favourite values

Here are some brilliant values that have had a pivotal role in changing the culture and fortunes of brands we have known or worked with.

Crustybusting: completely changed the culture and attitude to new product development at a brand that had a reputation for being a bit 'standoffish'.

Mateyness: this was one of four new values that helped drive a youth-targeted brand's product development and staff-recruitment strategies. The business nearly trebled in size in four years.

The Dungeons

Where to start?! The brand has a wonderfully differentiating set of values that we guarantee would not feature anywhere else, and the team there has made them resonate throughout the whole CX, even down to out-of-office messages:

> 'I have escaped the Dungeons for a whole week of daylight. I'll be returning to my torturing duties on Monday 13th March. Should you need assistance with anything scarily urgent, my fellow torturer Joe Bloggs is at your service.
> Have a horrible day!'

Wonderful!

Personality

As values are often mistaken for personality, so it also happens the other way around.

Personality has a very practical use; it should guide the way the brand speaks and acts. Think of it as the way it does things, not the what it does, as that is determined by its values and positioning.

If you go back to the newspaper example, it is easy to see that The Sun and The Times have different personalities. If you looked at nothing more than the way the headline is written, you would be able to guess the name of the newspaper from its tone and language. You might accuse us of using an obvious example, but nevertheless, to the CX Realist, this is heaven. No need to be clever for clever's sake.

Usually, two or three words, carefully chosen, can sum up the way a brand should talk, but the rules of 'stand out' versus 'foundation' that we outlined for values apply here as well.

Examples of brands with distinctive personalities include Ronseal, Paddy Power and Center Parcs.

Some companies have a unique way of expressing the personalities of their brands. They use a known personality or character to capture the personality of the whole brand (not just the way it talks), and this can be immensely powerful – imagine writing copy or developing training that uses Jack Nicholson as The Joker or Willy Wonka as your guide. It works, doesn't it?

Ensuring that there is a consistent interpretation of the personalities, especially when the brands are international, can be tricky, but when this is achieved, it works brilliantly.

Keeping personality real

We developed a personality for a national retailer using four words. It captured the distinct tone of voice and attitude to life that we wanted the brand to have, but we all thought it would help if we found a personality that captured it in a nutshell. We knew this would help interpretation across the business among the hundreds of people who were writing copy on behalf of the brand.

We chose 'Chris Evans on his breakfast show' as the guiding personality, and felt quite pleased that it captured the upbeat, positive attitude to life, the family values and the sunshine that he brought into people's mornings.

Well, that was the theory. The reality was very different. We undertook a roadshow of two-hour-long training sessions around the country with all the people who were writing copy, either in store, online, or for advertising, and found that it just didn't work. Despite the very specific reference to the element of his work we wanted to use, people could not get past his other work on TFI Friday, his old and long-passed boozy image or the fact that they just didn't like him. None of this should matter, but the CX Realist in us soon came to the conclusion that we had to go back to the six words.

Think about today's omnichannel environment. CX Realists know that personality is key, that all sorts of people need to use it and that simplicity and ease are crucial if you are to avoid looking schizophrenic.

Working out what the vision should be

Applying science to Visioning

The vision cannot be dreamt up on the laptop of a creative genius in the protected confines of their office in between games of table football. It has to be based in rigorous analysis: macro social and economic projections, data analysis, qualitative and quantitative assessment of the options and hard financial analysis of what can and cannot be delivered within the ambition and constraints of the business. In fact, all the stuff you should have found out in the Exploring stage.

No time for fluffiness here.

The centrepiece to establishing a vision is the Visioning workshop, but it is only part of an effective process.

It seems the word 'workshop' has become a much-maligned term and technique. We think that is probably because they often lack clear objectives, do not encourage the right behaviours and are not structured to within an inch of their lives (but in a way that no one would notice!).

The real question is who should attend a Visioning workshop? This is key. If the people at the top of the business are not involved, then forget it. CX development is transformational, it is focused on customers and the brand, the responsibility for which does not reside in one department and one department alone.

The new brand builders are the operation directors, human resources directors, FDs, MDs and CIDs. The burger seller.

And marketing.

The top people from all these areas need to be involved. They have hunches, long-held ideas and knowledge that must be incorporated in the process. They may have personal agendas and outdated ideas, too. A few also have huge egos and closed minds.

The resource needs to be tapped, minds opened, silos busted and egos managed.

Of course, that is often easier said than done. Some clients have suggested that we should 'avoid so and so because they are difficult', but this is exactly the thing you must not do. CX Realists will run towards this problem. They meet difficult people, spend time listening, gain their trust and reassure them that their contribution is critical. If someone can't make the Visioning workshop because they are 'too busy', respect this, see them one-to-one and make damn sure you report back. The CX Realist will make sure this happens, as they will recognise that, without the input, there is no chance.

Run at the problems

Operations directors in pub companies are tough – and understandably so. They tend not to like talking about brand or CX, as it's too 'fluffy wuffy', too much like marketing and just 'colouring in'. We once overheard the operations director for a big pub retailer say to a colleague, just before a session started, 'I just don't want to be here with these knobheads.' That was tough to take; we pretended we hadn't heard and, as CX Realists, we ran at the problem. It took some time, but we turned him around.

Another pub brand we were working with wanted to launch a whole new concept and needed a CX with consistent positioning, values and personality running through it. We worked directly with the operators, who made it work at breakneck pace because they believed in the process – and when an operations director charges at something, just watch a company shift. Transformation doesn't even begin to describe it.

One famous owner of a brand refused to attend a workshop. The only way we could see her was to join her on her cigarette break, which she enjoyed at hourly intervals outside her office. We kept her in the loop by travelling 70 miles both ways to wait for the 'fag break'. We then updated her on problems, outlined the barriers and asked for help where needed. These meetings happened in the rain, wind and snow (well, maybe not snow, but you get the picture).

Buy-in is earned. It cannot be demanded.

The workshop structure

The new vision for a brand will set the direction for a business. To be successful, it needs to have influences right across the business, so it stands to reason that the structure and facilitation of these sessions need preparation, stimulus and a load of experience.

Don't forget what works

We ran a workshop back in 2007 for a highly valued client and loved brand. It was a disaster. We did all the preparation work, gathered all the stimulus and then thought we would try out some new techniques because, frankly, we had become bored with the old ones.

Yes, that's the 'old ones' that we had developed over the previous seven years, that had been tried and tested and had proved to be effective. We forgot that the 'old ones' work, and while we keep on looking for improvement while practising the art of marginal gains, we know that we abandon those old ways at our peril. We still squirm at the memory.

Some tips for running a Visioning session for CX Realists

1. Nail the objective

The first thing here is to make sure that everyone knows what the objective is before you get to the workshop. This, of course, is another reason that you should see everyone before the session. Be clear, make sure you know what viewpoint there is of any existing vision, that you get hold of the business vision and know what the ambition for the business is so that you can work out the timelines and establish priorities.

The workshop objective is to develop a series of candidate brand visions – or, to be precise, no more than five different broad directions that the brand can go in.

The stage after this is to test options, both internally and externally, to see if they are compelling or not.

Visions were not built in a day

We were once challenged about this technique by the CEO of one of our clients. The challenge was that many companies force the team to come to a decision on the vision at the end of the session. In fact, they will not let the participants leave until they have all signed on the dotted line. This was the way that JWT ran its sessions in the 1990s, and the company took great pleasure in informing people that Day One could easily go into Day Two unless there was an agreement.

How can I put this politely?

What rubbish. That's as polite as I can get. If this technique is forced on you, please resist it at all costs. A vision agreed on the day will almost inevitably be a compromise, as it would have been completed under stress at the end of a long and tiring session and, critically, without the involvement of customers. What you need to do is agree on a shortlist of options to be tested with customers, both qualitatively and quantitatively.

Be careful what you throw away

At the end of a Visioning session for Blackpool (as a place brand), we had 14 potential directions. We managed to narrow them down to six to go into research, when someone suggested that we put in one of the rejected options as a clear differentiator from the rest, almost as fodder for the research. Of course, it won in research by a landslide and went on to guide the rejuvenation of the city (a massive long-term job), and still does to this day.

2. Bin jargon

CX Realists simply cannot go near jargon. It is one of the biggest barriers to overcome, as it creates confusion and reinforces silos. Sort out the jargon before you start, especially that around brands (often referred to by non-marketing people as 'brand bollocks', of course).

3. Keep reminding people that the vision is not a tagline!

We all do it. I know I do. We come up with a positioning option and then we turn it into something that sounds better or, dare I say it, is 'an advertising tagline'. Aargh! This is a nightmare. If it is a good one, it attracts attention in the session because it is a 'great line' rather than a great positioning, and it is likely to do well in research for the same reasons. Resist the temptation.

Visions with no vision

In one Visioning session, the creative director refused to work in a team when the options were being put together. He insisted on working on his own. At the end of the session, which, overall, had been a success, we agreed on four different directions for the brand. They were all expressed as simple sentences that captured exactly where the brand should sit. The creative director then insisted on giving us his. We all waited with bated breath while he took the stage:

'The brand is… dot, dot, dot.'

What the..?

It would appear that he was trying to write a tagline, and really his positioning was in the territory of 'imagination' and can be anything you want it to be – which is not much of a defining territory and definitely illustrates the dangers of tagline generation. Said creative director is still in place, but we do not exchange Christmas cards.

4.   Have a crystal-clear process

In the early days, when we worked with management consultants, we were constantly told that we have a lot of good theory, but the end result depends on a creative miracle. Well, this is anathema to most management consultants, and we had some sympathy with their view. In an attempt to add more science and process to Visioning, we added more data and research and developed a technique through which the options were developed.

Essentially, it starts with a territory, often expressed by one word. For example, Volvo is firmly in the 'safety' territory. There may be lots of territories and each one could give birth to a number of positions from within that territory. We then develop positionings around each territory, shortlist them and research qualitatively and quantitatively.

Territories to positioning

Let's have a look at theme parks – specifically, two within the Merlin Group: Thorpe Park and Alton Towers.

When we worked with Merlin on developing the Visions, a number of territories were available. After catchment profiling, visitor auditing, leisure-spend projections, brand auditing and a considerable amount of consumer research, two territories were developed: Thrill and Escape.

Two crystal-clear and differentiating Visioning statements were developed, which were visionary at the time (2007) and are shorthand for a longer positioning that includes all the proof points. They have never seen the light of day as a tagline, as they were never intended as such, but they have helped guide both brands in their development for 10 years. They have provided the lens through which the business was developed incredibly successfully over the past decade by the Merlin team.

Another example is the Millennium Wheel. That's what its working title was in 1998. After a visioning session that identified 'View' as its territory, the first thing that happened was the name changed and the fabulously successful and iconic London Eye was born. It all seems so obvious now, but at the time it could have gone in any number of directions.

5. Create a creative environment

It is always worth asking the workshop team to start thinking about their brand ahead of the session. We use an old technique to do this that involves attendees bringing along an item that captures what they think the brand should stand for in 10 years' time. We always encourage people to present their item right at the beginning of the workshop so that they are involved from the off and we can start building platforms from which the territories will evolve.

Icons for inspiration

At the Epsom Derby workshop, the then CEO brought along an indoor firework, which she proceeded to set alight. She thought the brand should be a 'celebration of summer'.

We held a Visioning workshop for a well-known optician where the MD brought along the great Louis Armstrong song What a Wonderful World to illustrate that the brand needed to be more emotional, less rational and should capture the joy of seeing.

What a Wonderful World by Louis Armstrong

I see trees of green,
red roses too.
I see them bloom,
for me and you.
And I think to myself,
what a wonderful world.

I see skies of blue,
And clouds of white.
The bright blessed day,
The dark sacred night.
And I think to myself,
What a wonderful world.

And those who can't be bothered just pretend that they brought their iPhone for this reason and talk about 'innovation' (there is always one).

6. Clearly communicate how to behave from the start

Folded arms. Frowns. Confusion.

Just a few of the things you can be faced with when running a Visioning workshop. You may have done all the right preparation, involved everyone in the process and stripped away the jargon, but you must always set the right tone and establish the best behaviours right from the start – warm them up at the beginning with some energiser techniques; there are loads on the internet.

We often ask people to write down their secret skill on a piece of paper, screw the paper up into a ball and throw it at us. We then all guess whose secret skill is whose. We have had international runners, people who can wrap their tongue around their nose and even porn stars! We use the same technique with 'first record ever bought' (I will have to change mine, as it is The Rip Offs play The Beatles – not cool). This year, we asked the participants at Home Group to tell us what they would do if they were king or queen for a day.

This is a fun exercise, but it also begins to get people to forget their day job, loosen up and enjoy what should be a great session.

Then we talk about nurturing ideas, staying in the sun and out of the rain, and we make sure that everyone feels comfortable.

7. Have clear judgment criteria

At the end of the session, there will be a number of candidate visions. At this stage, we need to narrow them down before they can formally be assessed, both internally and through research.

You can do this through voting (putting sticky stars on the favoured ones), but it is much better to have some clear criteria for assessment. These are the ones we use, and we assign marks out of 10 to each:

- How well does it align to the business strategy?
- How compelling is it to customers?
- How inspiring is it to the team?
- How differentiating is it?
- How easy is it to understand?
- How future proof is it?
- Will it drive action?
- How doable is it?

Testing the vision

There is no option for this. The vision needs to be tested, and tested rigorously – both qualitatively and quantitatively.

We have been handed visions by various companies over the years and asked to align it to their experience. Our first question is, 'What is the business ambition?' and our second is, 'Where is the evidence that this is right?'

Visions need to be practical

It came through the post.

Massive. We had to weigh it. It was a new brand vision for Somerfield (remember them?). It was a beauty. Reams of beautifully laid out pages illustrating and explaining a very lovely vision for the brand. It was good enough to put on your coffee table.

To be fair to Somerfield, they didn't really know what to do with it, and buried within it there may have been some genuine insight and genius positioning. But we couldn't find it and, crucially, there was no evidence that it was either compelling or doable.

Remember Somerfield?

Testing a vision is a specialist skill. You can't just lay all the options in front of people and take a vote. You need to understand why people are responding the way they do and you need to be sure that you know what they are responding to. Here are some top tips that apply equally to qualitative and quantitative vision testing.

Never test anything that looks like a tagline for research

It doesn't matter how many times you tell people it isn't a tagline, they will interpret it as such, and that could be very dangerous. The vision should be structured in a simple, logical pattern that can be repeated for each alternative, with only the key differences highlighted. This is especially critical in quantitative testing, when there is no chance to answer questions and ensure that people have understood.

Here is an example: in focus groups, ask respondents to create an imaginary high street with a number of alternative outlets/propositions, all equidistant from home (the key being to take geography out of the equation). Then ask the respondent to choose the proposition that they find most compelling. Here are some examples of the statements, all written in plain English:

1. This home-furnishing retailer is designed to allow you to express your creative side. It will give you

ideas that will help you create looks that you never thought possible.

2. This home-furnishing retailer is the cheapest in the market. It does not stock well-known brands and guarantees to be cheaper by at least 10%.

3. This home-furnishing retailer makes everything as easy as possible for you. It has all the well-known brands and the best service.

Layer the discussion so you know what people are responding to

This is more of a qualitative guide, although it does have quantitative implications.

There is probably a fancy research term for 'layering', but it will do for the CX Realist. The first layer of questioning would be around the general territory of the proposition, to see how compelling it is. You don't want to lose a great direction just because the specific wording isn't right. The next step is to hone in with a simple one-sentence proposition description, and then go into detail, showing examples and using stimulus, making sure all along that you know exactly what people are responding to.

Constantly check your interpretation and be prepared to change your approach as you go, as it may be a single word that is throwing an option off course and this could result in losing something that, expressed slightly differently, would be more positively received.

Equalise the stimulus

This applies both qualitatively and quantitatively, and it is a basic idea. Simply ensure you have equal quality and amount of stimulus for each option. For example, if you have put together a short video to demonstrate what one option might look like, make sure you have done the same for the others.

Envision the new omnichannel CX (bringing it to life once it's been tested)

Now it's time for some real excitement and to get a view and feel of what the new vision for the brand, translated into an omnichannel CX, could be like. This should be done at this point using film, illustration and storytelling, but only at the very top level as a form of stimulus (the detailed development should be completed later). When we have done this before, we have found that it whets people's appetites, inspires them and generates more support, enthusiasm and energy and allows ideas to be injected into the process early. It is well worth doing.

We created a short animated film for an international fitness brand that showed what a data-driven, omnichannel experience could look like for their customers. More than any statement, chart, list or weighty document, it became the one thing they shared with colleagues and always referred back to when there was disagreement or things felt that they were becoming too difficult. It encapsulated the reasons they were going on the CX transformational journey and reminded them what was and wasn't important.

Great visions

Great visions can be transformational. It is difficult here to share many of the great ones, as that would break client confidences, but to help illustrate what can work, here are a few and a view on why they work.

Starbucks famously set out the vision to be the *'third place in people's lives'* (after the office and home). This, along with its values, firmly established the goal to develop a very emotional relationship with its customers that engendered a strong sense of belonging. This will have directed the décor, recruitment training, policies and the service style, right down to the more recent introduction of writing first names on coffee cups and the app that allows you to pre-order your drink.

Britain's Greatest Escape is the brand vision for Alton Towers. It has remained untouched since 2007 and, in its full form (about eight words), sets out an easily usable but inspiring vision that aligns with the business ambition for the brand. Each word is important, as it determines the geographical reach, builds on its all-round proposition, history and its position as the market leader while focusing on the need for people to get away from the everyday. This vision has provided the foundation for new product development, the style and language of communications, service style, recruitment, training and provides a guide to what the brand should and shouldn't do throughout the whole CX.

Immediate Freedom for Everyone was the vision used by Hertz for its development of a short-term car-rental proposition similar to Zipcar or Streetcar. Again, each word was carefully chosen and aligned with the corporate ambition and market trends.

Turning the words into action

At this point, everything humanly possible has been done to make Exploring and Visioning 'real'. The truth has been hunted down, people throughout the company have been involved, customers have been interrogated, hard data and testing have been used to prove and disprove theories, and fancy-pants language has been avoided. All the work will have been done in full consciousness of the real business and market environment, and all the omnichannel options have been explored. Throughout all this, the true hardcore Realist will be fighting the urge to actually change something and see it in action. Calm yourself, hardcore Realists – the time has come. Let's hear from the man himself:

> *"Vision without action is merely a dream. Action without vision is just passing time. Vision with action can change the world."*
> NELSON MANDELA

Visioning: what's hot and what's not

Hot	Not
Developing a vision to act as the lens for what you do and don't do	Just doing stuff with no big picture in sight
Creating the vision by balancing the needs and capability of the business with the customers' needs and desires	Forgetting the business reality
Making the vision visionary	Staying in the here and now
Collaboratively developing the vision with those who will be responsible for delivering it	Creating another silo and all the defensiveness and resistance that comes with it
Using simple, everyday language	Using pseudo-intellectual twaddle that looks clever but is completely useless in reality
Making it compelling and inspiring	Uninspiring and samey-samey
Being clear about what the vision is supposed to do and how it differs from the business vision	Leaving it to chance and creating confusion
Having stand-out values that differentiate	Having values that make no difference
Testing quantitatively and qualitatively, internally and externally	Sticking your finger in the air
Storytelling to inspire the team(s)	Not capitalising on the excitement and engagement that the process brings

3. ALIGNING

"When you have superb alignment, a visitor could drop into your organisation from another planet and infer the vision without having to read it on paper."
JIM COLLINS AND JERRY I PORRAS

CX Realists, this really is your moment. Customer Experience is the future battleground, where business success will be determined, fortunes won and lost. Many companies will prioritise the continual improvement of their CX. Pain points will be eliminated, efficiencies made and satisfaction improved.

The picture we paint is not of the distant future, of course – it is happening already, and when we go to conferences we see fantastic presentations from companies, often in the same sector, who are doing exactly the same things to improve their CX. This often leads to our standard question: 'How will you remain different and more compelling than your competitors?' This question is regularly met with silence and not a little annoyance. It hits a nerve. As we said in the introduction, the difference in the approach we are describing is that it uses the brand to drive success. The Aligning stage is where it comes to the fore and you make it happen.

It's not just us saying this. Martin Glenn, in his last speech as CEO of United Biscuits, described the future as 'all about the A word'. Aligning the brand's positioning, values and personality through the CX is already making the difference for a number of highly successful companies and organisations. The beauty of the approach is that it costs no more than not aligning, it isn't rocket science and it has so many other benefits. Logically, then, it won't be long before everyone is doing it this way.

Aligning is the key difference in this approach, and it could make a big difference for you. You only need to do the Exploring and Visioning so you can define the opportunities to make your CX compelling. You need the brand to drive it all. If Exploring and Visioning have already been done well, you can proceed to the important bit. You use those two elements to figure out what the brand needs to do now and in the future. This is Alignment, and it is what matters and what makes you different.

Before we start sharing some Aligning experiences and outline a way to do it, let's revisit how it works and why it is so important.

The Aligning narrative

Back in our Mad Men days of the 1990s, it was drummed into us that whatever the client's problem, the answer was always 'advertising'. If the problems were bigger, then the answer simply required bigger budgets. What a simple world it was.

This always troubled us hugely, as it obviously wasn't the case – you couldn't advertise yourself out of everything. Even in the 90s, we had no way of articulating a different solution, and we sure as hell couldn't make any money out of anything other than ads.

Then, in 1990, we were lucky enough to win a pitch that changed our way of thinking and effectively changed our lives. The pitch was for a famous but declining theme park near Stoke-on-Trent called Alton Towers. The marketing director at the time was Nick Varney, now CEO of Merlin Entertainments. Nick was and still is a visionary, and he encouraged us to get involved beyond the normal remit of an ad agency. He invited us to contribute across the whole customer experience because that, he believed, was the way brands were built (there was no UX at the time). In effect, he was a pioneering omnichannellist (phew, what a word; we won't be using it again).

In what was a major brand-repositioning programme, we helped, with varying levels of involvement, to realign the company culture, new product development, entertainments and the processes that ran the park. We loved it, even though we were sometimes only on the periphery of what was a revolution in branding. In the late 90s, Nick introduced us to this quote by Michael Eisner, former CEO of Disney, which captures the way Nick thinks about brands. It's still our mantra today – we probably use it in 50% of presentations and 100% of pitches that we do (thanks, Nick). It's a classic and worth absorbing and thinking about.

'Frank and I soon recognised something that could be achieved in a single broad stroke. We came to think of Disney as a canvas on which many artists paint in pointillist style – one dot at a time. If each of those dots is executed with precision, imagination, and an awareness of the whole, the painting becomes richer, more vibrant and multidimensional. Walt Disney and his team created such a masterpiece. When a new group of artists comes along, the risk is that they bring a diminished commitment to excellence, or a lack of attention to the whole. Then the opposite process can occur. Point by point, stroke by stroke, the masterpiece deteriorates into something mediocre and commonplace, even ugly, until eventually destroyed altogether. A brand is a living entity, and it is enriched or undermined cumulatively over time, the product of a thousand small gestures.'
Michael Eisner, CEO, Disney, 1984–2005

There is so much in this Eisner quote. Among many things, it brilliantly articulates how the whole business is involved in brand building, not just the designers and marketers. For some makers of ads, logos and design, this can be a tricky thing to take on board, as they once considered themselves the guardians of the brand; the natural occupants of a place on the board, with the ear of the CEO and the drivers of brand strategy. This mentality is less common now, but while the bow ties may have disappeared from the boardroom, the narrow thinking in advertising, brand consultancies, design agencies and media companies sometimes remains.

There are, of course, notable exceptions to this, but in the many meetings we have that involve these types of supplier companies, some of which are massive global operators, we often find ourselves having to argue the case that 'brands are built by experience, so let's look at that before we shoot the 60-second commercial in Mauritius'. It can still be a tricky sell.

"The challenging thing in retailing is that your customers experience your product directly. They actually walk through the store for an hour every week. That has much more impact than any amount of media advertising. What they experience in the store is the brand. So stores have to be both internally and externally coherent."
Archie Norman, Ex-Chairman, ASDA

Hallelujah!

The new order

In the ads-versus-experience debate, it is an easy win for the Realists. It is done and dusted as an argument, unless you are a dreamer, of course.

"In the old world, you devoted 30% of your time to building great service and 70% of your time shouting about it. In the new world, that inverts."
Jeff Bezos, CEO, Amazon

"68% of people tell others about brilliant customer experiences; 48% won't buy from brands if a friend has had a bad experience."
Brand Vista, 2016

This revolution was started by technology and continued by consumers who have grown wise and sceptical. They know their power and they share the good, the bad and the ugly elements of their customer experiences on a monumental scale. More than ever, consumers demand greater involvement, customisation, personalisation and mobility from services – with immediate results. When they see cutting-edge service innovations in one industry, they expect to find them in others as well (Service Innovation in a Digital World, McKinsey, 2015). Consumers are having their day; the Mad Men have had theirs.

As if this weren't enough to contend with, the competitive landscape has exploded. Companies now find themselves compared with brands outside their category or geography, while at the same time having to raise standards as expectations go up, up and up again. The benchmark criteria in whatever market you are in may be set by Amazon for service and efficacy, Uber for ease of use and budget hotels for value delivered. It almost seems unfair.

"The days of brands competing with other brands within category is over. Customers will compare the experience they have within the automotive category to that of supermarkets, hotels and sports brands. The customer experience that brands deliver will differentiate them from one another."
Laura Schwab, Marketing Director, Land Rover

With so much supporting evidence, it's no surprise that CX-led improvement has fast become a central objective of business around the world and that, everywhere you go, you bump into CX people. They come from all sorts of different categories and disciplines: customer services, insight, marketing (obviously), digital, user experience, e-commerce, call-centre management, training, business improvement, quality and many others.

In 2000, we came out.

Seeing 'the CX light' in 2000 but not really knowing what it was or what to call it, we left JWT, formed Brand Vista and called what we did 'brand alignment'. Put simply, this was the alignment of compelling positioning, the values and personality of a brand through the whole Customer Experience (CX).

Calling it 'brand alignment' wasn't our best move. No one was listening; it was a tough sell. Then, in the late 2000s, we noticed that others were calling what we do 'customer experience'. This was a great moment for us, if a little annoying, but it didn't take much time for us to work out that a lot of the talk around CX development did not involve the brand – most of it revolved around 'improvement'. This puzzled us, as merely improving the customer experience does not necessarily make it compelling, irresistible or, dare we say, 'hot'. We had been saying for many years that the brand is the key to all this and it should be used to drive a compelling CX. Branding has not gone away – in fact, it has never been more important, but the method by which you 'brand' has changed dramatically.

Hot CX is more than just 'improvement'

When CX first hit the news, the metrics used to measure CX success typically focused on efficiency gains, reduced friction and resource savings. As we said in the introduction, these are highly prized and difficult-to-achieve improvements but, as more and more companies 'improve' their CX, the more homogenous they become; what is seen as differentiating one month becomes standard practice the next.

Making a difference

In autumn 2016, we attended a CX conference in London where the speakers shared the ways in which they had cut waste, reduced friction and improved satisfaction. A high proportion of presenters were from the financial sector – many from banks – and they all said virtually the same thing. This is all well and good – these are key elements of CX design – but without the differentiating and consumer-focused guidance of the brand, everyone will end up in exactly the same place, with a few notable exceptions. Without a compelling brand, nobody will perceive any differences in a commodity sector, and customers may even forget who they bank with.

The forward-thinking CX Realist is well aware that a different approach will be required if their CX is to remain compelling, drive differentiation, maintain customer focus, inspire the internal team and drive success in whatever form it takes.

This approach requires an entirely different mindset, *an Aligning mindset.*

In practical terms, this means hot-wiring the proposition, values and personality of the brand throughout the CX, thus providing a guide as to what the brand should and should not do, the way it is delivered and the inspiration and focus for innovation. This keeps it compelling, differentiating, customer focused and internally inspiring.

Uniting the Xs

Our favourite example showcasing the degree to which the UX/CX separation can exist is from a very large national retailer with whom we have worked for four years.

If you happened to visit its headquarters you could turn left from reception into the 'store side', where you were met with formality and suits, or you could turn right into the UX world, where it was all flip flops, shorts in the summer and table football. The two sides kept themselves to themselves (in fact, there was open hostility between them), and they didn't see this divide as either weird or counterproductive.

To us, it is both – and the most crucial thing is that customers do not see two different sides. It's one brand to them. Of course it is!

The CX vs UX debate – a cabby's view

One of the first things we need to sort out is exactly what channels we are aligning. Many companies believe that the digital experience (so-called UX) and the physical experience (CX) should be treated separately. So, let's get this straight: the UX/CX divide is rubbish. Hot CX treats the entire customer experience, both digital and physical 'sides', as one. It's the omnichannel approach and it's just how the consumer sees it.

As evidence, m'lord, let me present the case of Moose Cabs (not their real name, but the story is real and based on a taxi company in Hertfordshire).

We recently had the opportunity to visit Hatfield on a fairly regular basis to attend meetings with one of our newest clients, David Lloyd Leisure. The company's HQ is at a David Lloyd club – a brilliant club that I can highly recommend, but it's too far from the station to walk, so we take a taxi every time.

We ordered a taxi on my smartphone where the so-called UX blew my mind. I received a text telling me that my taxi was on time, what colour the car was, the registration plate and the name of the driver. Magnificent. When I reordered my taxi, it intuitively stored my frequent journeys and asked me to select which one I needed now. Genius! It even sent me a nice little thank you.

Fantastic UX. It couldn't have been easier or more insightful. Cigar time.

So, how are things in the Moose Cabs CX department?

Subsequent journeys saw the taxi consistently turning up at the wrong door to pick me up, meaning I had to call to ask them specifically to go to the office entrance – and they still haven't got it right. The walk isn't long between the two entrances, but certainly long enough to get soaking wet in our British weather. Also, should I ever run even a minute late, I am told that 'waiting charges will be incurred'. To add to this, the drivers are not Hatfield's finest – they are probably the grumpiest, most non-conversant set of drivers this side of Moscow, and the cars are old and tatty.

It's a thumbs down for the Moose Cabs CX department.

The lesson here is that, as a customer, it felt like I was dealing with two completely different companies. I went from CX to UX to CX to UX and back to CX. There was no unified experience and definitely no alignment to the brand (the Moose Cabs vision is to be the most personal cab company in the world –they have been reading Jim Collins).

OK, small-scale stuff, you may argue, but the same thing happens in big, multi-billion-pound companies every day.

So, to paraphrase Castlemaine XXXX: 'All this UX and CX discrimination is XXXX to us.' Whether it's face to face, over the phone or online, they are all just other channels; part of the series of touchpoints among the thousands that build brands. We predict that soon it will sort itself out and everything will come under the CX banner.

Or, in other words, companies will put all their 'X' in one basket. Ahem.

Evidence that it works.
We touched on some of the evidence earlier in the book and hardly a day or conference goes by that doesn't produce more research and facts to prove the point that CX is the business battleground. Here are three of our current favourites:

- 'A 2% increase in customer retention has the same effect as decreasing costs by 10%.' (Leading on the Edge of Chaos, Emmett Murphy and Mark Murphy, 2002)

- '70% of buying decisions are based on how the customer feels.' (18 Interesting Stats to Get You Rethinking Your Customer Service Process, McKinsey cited in salesforce.com, 2013)

- 'According to a CEI Survey, 86% of buyers will pay more for a better customer experience, but only 1% feel that companies consistently meet their expectations.' (Customer Experience: Is It the Chicken or Egg?, Forbes, 2013)

Aligning for Hot CX

We hope that we have proved that aligning makes the difference. If you believe it, then the next stage becomes a moment of truth as you create a CX that aligns with the brand vision.

Surprising aligning

Aldi and Lidl are kings of alignment. When we use them as examples of aligned brands, people often scoff and start arguing. Now, we are always up for a debate, but the simple, brutal truth here is that these brands set out very clearly what they are and take an omnichannel approach to deliver it at every touchpoint. By doing this, they deliver exactly to expectations. Their positioning, values and personality are hardwired throughout everything they do, through the thousands of small gestures, and, unsurprisingly, they are succeeding, stealing share and are very happy, thank you very much.

Perhaps it's not surprising to see Pret A Manger, Pets at Home and First Direct among our list of great purveyors of Hot CX. They are easier to 'like' personally, but the point is they don't have to be aspirational to be Hot, and it is all about compelling alignment to a vision that is right for the business, delivered through an omnichannel approach.

Hot CX in the air

We considered leaving Ryanair out of Hot CX, given its 2017 difficulties with pilot holiday rostering that forced it to cancel thousands of flights, but we decided to include it as it is such a good example of alignment. There is no getting away from the fact that it was seamlessly aligned, as the values, personality and proposition ran through every touchpoint. Admittedly, time is now catching up with it, the consumer is changing and Ryanair is having to relax the brutality of the alignment – but, let's face it, the company continues to grow despite the difficulties.

On the other hand, as of 2017, you could argue that British Airways has not aligned its brand and is suffering for it. Good service, high levels of integrity and 'Britishness' have been left behind in the battle with the discounters, and suddenly consumers no longer know what they are getting. It is misaligned and meandering aimlessly... or so it may seem to us as passengers.

Envisioning the aligned CX

If you have belief in this approach, you will agree that if your brand vision is to be 'Britain's Greatest Escape' or your essence is 'liberating freedom' or your core value is 'clubbiness', then you have to deliver it at the points in the customer journey where it matters most.

Let's face it – if you don't find this bit exciting, it's time to leave it all behind and set sail on that round-the-world trip you have always fancied; this world isn't for you. So let's gather the Exploring output, the existing CX journey map and your compelling new vision and start envisioning. There are two ways to do it.

1. Give creatives freedom

There is always value in giving creative professionals time and resources to use their knowledge, the Exploring stimulus and their unique way of thinking to take the vision and think of ideas outside of workshop environments. Leave them alone for a few days to imagine, dream and create. The brand vision will guide and inspire them, but it should not constrain them – you can apply the brand-vision filter and the practicalities later.

Letting creatives 'go it alone' for a while will allow them to use their skills to the fullest; they will not have to jump through workshop hoops and they will not be subdued by the presence of their clients. They will give you ideas and open up possibilities that you probably didn't even know existed and can inject elements that can prove genuinely different, especially as they are not weighed down with the knowledge of what has worked or not worked in the past. History can be a burden.

The downside is client buy-in can be more difficult to get afterwards, but this can be overcome by using the creatives' output as stimulus and seeding in the workshops to let the group debate it and start to own it.

2. Workshops

The other way to do this is to apply some of the principles from earlier and, through a series of workshops, engage with the top team and others who have fertile, innovative minds and the ability to think differently. Make sure you plan well, have big, airy, sunlit rooms and that you create an environment and atmosphere in which innovation can flourish. They will be some of the best 'work' days you'll ever have.

3. Wear your brand goggles

There are so many things that need improving in any CX that it is easy to fall into the trap of focusing on these alone and sidelining the brand. Of course, creating an 'improved CX' will bring good benefits, but not great long-term benefits – after all, it's not 'hot'.

The way to keep the brand central is to give everyone a pair of 'brand goggles'. The goggles act as the lens through which to envision the future-facing CX. It can simply be the brand written on one page or an actual pair of goggles with the vision attached in some way.

Our first CX mapping exercise was awful, but we learned a lot.

We plotted a household-name brand CX with a team of 15 people who represented all parts of the business. As we were going through the process, we soon realised that we were making improvements to many things, but neither the brand nor its customers were central. Try as we might, we couldn't keep the brand central. We then invented the 'brand goggles' and, a couple of weeks later, repeated the exercise at another brand. As we completed our walk-through of the experience, we were able to shorthand the brand vision in a simple, consumable way by simply asking people to 'put their goggles on'.

It worked a treat.

David Lloyd actually made the goggles and used them to launch the whole programme. We have goggles with flashing lights, Las Vegas-style goggles for Gala Bingo, and beer goggles (naturally) for a pub brand we work with.

4. Do it with feeling – use customer feelings as the guide for your envisioned CX

Another way to keep your CX hot is to make feelings central. We know that emotional connections are very powerful, so we need to ask ourselves, at every stage, what are the feelings that we need to deliver?

> *"I've learned that people will forget what you said, people will forget what you did, but people will never forget how you made them feel."* - MAYA ANGELOU

Doing it this way has proven financial benefits. The Harvard Business Review researched the feelings associated with brands. The research was as robust as research can be (it is Harvard, after all), and they isolated the top-10 feelings associated with brands that correlate with business value. Effectively, the research directly links emotions to money.

I am inspired by a desire to:	Brands can leverage this motivator by helping customers:
Stand out from the crowd	Project a unique social identity. Be seen as special.
Have confidence in the future	Perceive the future as better than the past; have a positive mental picture of what's to come.
Enjoy a sense of wellbeing	Feel that life measures up to expectations and that balance has been achieved; seek a stress-free state without conflicts or threats.
Feel a sense of freedom	Act independently, without obligations or restrictions.
Feel a sense of thrill	Experience visceral, overwhelming pleasure and excitement; participate in exciting, fun events.
Protect the environment	Sustain the belief that the environment is sacred; take action to improve their surroundings.
Be the person I want to be	Fulfil a desire for ongoing self-improvement; live up to their ideal self-image.
Feel secure	Believe that what they have today will be there tomorrow; pursue goals and dreams without worry.
Succeed in life	Feel that they lead meaningful lives; find worth that goes beyond financial or socioeconomic measures.

Source: Scott Magids, Alan Zorfas and Daniel Leemon
From: The New Science of Customer Emotions, 2015

In touch with their feelings

Putting a roof over someone's head and helping them to find the care that they need is a high-level mission, especially when the people involved are vulnerable. One of our clients does this very thing, and plotting the feelings that are key across the whole CX covered seven of the top-10 feelings in Harvard's list. If the company gets it right at the appropriate stages, it will build immense value, while at the same time helping a lot of people.

One of our Venture Capital (VC) clients has 'clubbiness' as a brand value. One of the feelings this evokes is belonging. Knowing that it correlates with a company value helped the team at our client sell the process to their owners, who could then be more easily convinced that the seemingly 'fluffy' notion of plotting feelings had financial rewards. In other words, 'there is hard cash in the soft stuff'.

5. Keep looking ahead
The 'here and now' can often get in the way.

A media client was desperately trying to break from the shackles of the 'here and now' to work out its future vision, which is tricky but essential if you are to have an 'envisioned vision' and not just a mirror of what you already have. One tip we used to help them was to look so far ahead that it makes the 'here and now' and the 'just over the horizon' thinking redundant. So, rather than a five-year horizon, go for 20. It doesn't always work, but it can dig you out of the 'here and now' hole.

6. Brand – the big basics

Within every CX there are basics of delivery. These are things that have to be done – the hygiene factors, if you like. The envisioned CX needs to capture and improve them. It is essential that this happens, but there will be certain basics that you can alight to your brand and deliver in a compelling, differentiating way.

Compelling brand basics

Premier Inn is a great example of what it means to make a brand basic compelling. Premier Inn is a fantastically successful, no-frills budget hotel brand, and you could argue that the foundation of this success is that it identified a universal customer expectation – a basic of delivering a good night's sleep – and delivers this in a uniquely aligned way.

The hotel chain centres its experience on this basic. It claims to have the best pillows, it has great beds, it gives you good sleep tips and its 'Good Night Guarantee' is a simple, scalable and consistent reinforcement of the brand promise. If you don't have a good night's sleep, you can claim your money back.

Like millions of others, we have put the Premier Inn promise to the test – and the company keeps it.

Premier Inn is Hot CX.

Until you get your basics sorted, you should forget trying to do anything special. If the basics aren't well executed, they can create huge frustrations and really rile customers up, demonstrating that the brand really doesn't give a monkey's about them, it just wants to show off to competitors.

Employees can also become fed up and irritated when the basics are not delivered well. They tell us of speeches from senior people proudly talking about new initiatives, when nothing is happening to help them do the basic jobs that customers expect and demand.

It is brand critical to build your brand basics into the envisioned CX from the very start, that you prioritise the ones that really matter and then deliver them in a brand-driven way.

Interestingly, in many sectors, if all you did was deliver on your brand basics 'in an aligned way', you would have a differentiated brand. We did this with a famous retail client and it went from number two to number one in revenue terms in just six months.

Get basic

A large grocer we worked with had grand ambitions about misting machines, digitally enabled aisles, in-store mobile games and automated traffic-flow management. But the aisles were often poorly stocked, and a number of stores weren't always cleaned very well. None of the innovations could impress as long as the basics weren't in place. The CEO lost his job over it, and now the basics have been fixed.

7. Amplify your brand

There will be times in the CX when you can amplify your brand with moments of innovation that are aligned to your brand.

Hot CX demands this.

Brand Amplifiers, as we call them (you may call them Moments of Magic, or Wow Moments), are central to creating a compelling and differentiating CX.

Some people have described these as indulgent interactions that have limited longer-term value, despite getting a huge number of hits on social media and praise in marketing circles. The Realist would say that these moments in a customer's journey should exist only if they amplify the brand and inspire customers to become part of the communication effort of the business.

A top tip here is to get the right team together and run a special Brand Amplifier session using a tightly and well-researched session plan and some specialist innovation techniques. You will need loads of stimulus from around the world to create an environment and atmosphere where innovation can flourish. Lots of energy-boosting exercises and the right people in the room are also essential.

8.   Check the temperature – is it hot or not?

Sticking to the evidence-based approach means that whatever envisioned customer experience the team has come up with should be tested with customers, to ensure that it is compelling, motivating and, in a word, 'hot'.

For one client, we took 12 Brand Amplifiers to test with customers. Our client thought they had created some big Wow Moments, but customers thought otherwise. The ideas were compelling, but as Basics, not Amplifiers. That's the thing about customers: they can be very brutal about what they expect. It surprised the client and resulted in a few other Amplifiers being developed and the rest joining the Basics list.

Testing is fantastic. Bringing the Amplifiers to life visually, whether with text, pictures or digital prototypes, enables you to probe and discuss what works and what doesn't and often results in an amalgamation or further development of specific Amplifiers. In fact, we'd contest that nothing is more powerful than prototypes, both as stimulus and in making us all see that the Amplifier is real, which makes it much more likely to actually happen.

And sometimes, you just get it completely wrong.

Identifying Amplifiers

We were working for a national bookmaker with more than 500 branches, where our insight discovered that customers new to placing bets, especially women, found bookmakers intimidating. One solution, seen internally as a Brand Amplifier, was to introduce a 'meeter and greeter' at each branch. This tested appallingly. The last thing people wanted was to be spoken to as they walked in – it would have actively turned them off.

For a building client, we tested an Amplifier that put all the local knowledge of an area in an app, so you could check out the bus routes, local schools, pubs and so on in one place. In the general discussion, the Amplifier was largely dismissed, but after the digital prototype had been shown, it emerged as one of the top-three ideas.

We developed an idea for a large ice-cream manufacturer to turn the tops of ice-cream freezer cabinets into gaming screens that would attract people into shops and aligned perfectly with the playful brand. Customers loved it, too, but as soon as we spoke to shop owners, they were very clear that the last thing they needed was kids filling up their shops and stopping others from getting to the ice creams.

How Ladies' Day at Aintree Racecourse did it: Amplification from deep insight

One potent Brand Amplifier that played a significant part in re-energising the relationship between a company and its customers was recently launched at Aintree Racecourse for Ladies Day' at the Grand National Festival.

Historically, guests would be filtered and hustled through turnstiles in order to control them, but these ladies were dressed exquisitely from head to toe, ready to spend money and have an amazing time – how could this be better aligned to the brand? The answer was to make them feel like Hollywood stars. The turnstiles were replaced by a red carpet, while newly appointed 'Racemakers' welcomed the ladies in and set the tone for the day as a celebration. The Twittersphere went crazy, Instagram exploded and, together, Aintree Racecourse and Brand Vista reset the benchmark for making Ladies' Day a unique and memorable occasion.

9.   Engage, engage, engage

You can't base your envisioned CX on just one workshop or meeting with the top team – far from it. This would be a missed opportunity of the highest order. This is the chance to engage people from across the organisation, often for the first time, to nail what needs to be done and what is possible.

If involvement is restricted to the top team, you will only achieve a view far removed from the customer and employee experience; if, however, it's too frontline, your view will not be end-to-end and problems and opportunities will be missed. The Realist will engage a wider group and achieve a balanced view.

The envisioned CX: a summary

Today's customers expect a fast, agile, constantly evolving and improving customer experience, be they B2B, B2C or, indeed, B2B2C, and the business expects a return for its efforts based on empirical returns and not just customer satisfaction. In other words, we need to be able to pat our head and rub our tummies at the same time.

The envisioned omnichannel CX provides the detail of how a company is going to interact with customers in a way that is aligned to the vision for the brand. It outlines the feelings the brand seeks to deliver at each touchpoint, based around the jobs that customers need to do.

It must seamlessly align the digital and physical parts of the CX to the vision for the brand, which, in turn, should be aligned to the vision for the business.

Its objective will be to remove friction for customers and also the people serving them, ensuring the basic requirements are identified and the key ones done in the brand's own unique way. It must also identity the moments where you can amplify the brand and stand out.

Hot CX uses the brand vision as a lens through which the business can align touchpoints that deliver the right first impressions, friction-free movement and lasting impressions as they pass through each interaction.

Aligning: what's hot and what's not

Hot	Not
Using the vision to create a compelling omnichannel CX	Improving only one channel
Using the brand as a lens through which you decide what to do and what not to do	Having no lens – just doing what looks good
Using the brand to guide the ways in which you do things	Delivering in an differentiated way
Using customers' needs and desires as the framework for development	Using customers' needs and desires as the framework for development
Identifying the basics of the category and applying the brand vision to the key ones	Identifying the basics of the category and applying the brand vision to the key ones
Identifying the most effective touchpoints in the CX to amplify the brand	Trying to amplify everything
Trying to amplify everything	Not trying to differentiate
Testing to see what is hot and what is not	Using a finger-in-the-air approach

4. DELIVERING

"You are defined by what you do, not what you say you are going to do."
CARL JUNG

My dad is old school. A printer by trade his whole life, with one job at one company, and never a day off work. When he asks me what I do for a living, he is really asking me 'what do you make?' In other words, what is it that we produce that people want to buy? For years, this has been a question I have dreaded. My response could take hours, as his questions – doused in scepticism – piled in one after the other, and my laboured answers, accidentally laced with jargon, got more and more desperate and exasperated. It's Venus and Mars. It happens a couple of times a year; you have probably been there yourself. It's even worse with the children.

But now we have an answer that will make these conversations a whole lot easier: we make customer experiences – and everybody needs a good one, or they will soon be history.

Until we have delivered the CX successfully, we haven't really done very much at all. All the robust, insightful Exploring, Visioning and Aligning means nothing until we have delivered a compelling experience that generates business. At this point we need to come clean: we have helped a few businesses do all the hard work to get to the Delivering stage, only to see the plans end up purely as part of a sale prospectus or abandoned by new people coming into the business who have seen things differently. That said, when it goes well, it is fantastic and a little humbling.

Delivering is where all the hard work comes to life – for the people of the business and its customers, current and future. It turns strategy into action and action into a communication medium that develops stronger bonds inside and outside the business. However, not everyone gets it right, and only a few get it right all the time, so let's explore Delivering and the things that make it work – and

102

the things that get in the way.

The assets you need to deliver Hot CX

Throughout the Delivering process, you need a full set of Hot CX assets:

- The brand vision in terms of the visionary positioning, the values that drive brand behaviours, the personality that defines how it does things and its tone of voice.

- The envisioned CX, shaped by the brand vision and informed through Exploring.

- The omnichannel Brand Basics of the category and how you will deliver the key ones in alignment with the vision.

- The Brand Amplifiers that represent real innovation for the brand and maintain its differentiation.

- The support of the senior team and their buy-in and empowering support.

- The support of the frontline teams whose involvement has helped shaped the CX across all the touchpoints.

Delivering Hot CX

Since 2000, when we left the Mad Men world and started helping companies use their brands to deliver Hot CX, we have experienced both success and failure. The lessons we have learned in this time have been mastered the hard way, and there have been many challenges that have accelerated our understanding and helped us focus on the 'real worldliness' that is needed to succeed. We have pooled our understanding and isolated a number of Critical Success Factors that typify the successes, and tried to identify what gets in the way of success.

The critical success factors

1.   Get the right people on the bus

In his book *Good to Great*, Jim Collins created a memorable metaphor by comparing business to a bus and the leader as the bus driver. His first guiding principle is the need to 'get the right people on the bus'. His second is to get the right people in the right seats. This metaphor could have been developed for Hot CX, especially when the work required to develop it successfully is likely to be transformational and will require key people to work in fresh and inspiring ways.

Creating Hot CX requires a mix of people from across the business who are either actively involved themselves or have committed their team to it. At the very least they need to believe in its importance as a priority to the business. Getting the support of the right people will be much easier if you have conducted the first three Hot CX stages in the collaborative, engaging and inspiring way we recommend, have run at any barriers with openness, enthusiasm and humility, and proven the worth to the business. If you have done it this way you will be off to a flying start, and even though you can never totally relax, people will be clambering to get on the bus, as it will be seen to be going places. When this happens, Hot CX will become a real possibility.

So, think carefully about who joins the bus – you will need a team with clout and desire from a number of departments:

- **Operations**. This is key to the success of Hot CX. Operators make things happen and can stop a programme in its tracks. Get them onside and, wow – watch it go! They will move mountains. Leave them off the bus, though, and see the brakes come on…

- **Human resources**. Despite the relentless march of the digital age, Hot CX will always require people to deliver it at some point. Colleagues need to be aligned to the brand, inspired and enthused. HR know their way around a business, direct recruitment, training and reward and recognition, and regardless of whether the CX is physical or digitally led, their involvement is key. Free up a seat.

- **Finance**. Money makes the world go round, and it also fuels the bus. You might think that convincing Finance of the importance of delivering Hot CX could be more difficult than explaining to your children what it is you do – less Venus and Mars and more Venus and Pluto. You imagine it's a case of different languages and different psyches, but that is not our experience. Hot CX delivers savings, greater efficiency, improvements that correlate with business success and quantifiable sales results. Financiers obviously respond to that, and you need them to be on-side.

Show me the money

Efficiency savings: once the CX has been aligned to the vision, it is possible to identify 'pain' points and take targeted appropriate action that enhances the CX, thereby making significant savings:

- £1 million saved for a world-famous media brand in the first year of transformation, with a further £2 million saving accrued a year later
- £2.9 revenue, £1.6 million cost savings and 112,000 hours back to an online retailer in 2016
- £11,000 spent on a one-pilot programme, with benefits of £60,000 cost savings, plus undisclosed revenue increases for a distribution company

However, it's not all plain sailing with Finance. On 12 September 2001, we had scheduled a meeting with the CEO of a global investment company. This, of course, was the day after the attack on the Twin Towers, and the world was absorbing and digesting the tragic news. As he had time on his hands, we ended up in a heated four-hour debate that should have lasted five minutes. We were arguing the importance of customer experience (by the way, note the year is 2001), and he was adamant that customers didn't matter; it was the numbers that counted. The quite simple correlation between happy customers who keep coming back and tell their friends how good something is and good numbers was completely lost on him. No matter what we said. However, we argued it, he just wouldn't see our point of view. The shame was he is just the kind of person who needs to be on the bus – the manager of fuel, without whom the chances of achieving Hot CX are, at best, lukewarm. As we said, this was 16 years ago – perhaps he'd think differently now.

- **Information technology.** Rather than being siloed and treated more as a production department than brand and CX builders, IT need to have a seat on the bus, as exposure to the wider thinking of what the company is doing is essential. This way, they can see the impact of their work and the ways in which the digital journey is only part of the whole and not its sum. This has enormous benefits, as it will eventually reduce much of the mutual suspicion that both the physical and digital sides of a business sometimes have for each other, meaning they will work together better and results will come more quickly.

  Often, companies can be led by the latest bit of sexy equipment the IT team presents to them, whether it's right for the brand or not. Having them on the bus will ensure they can make the most appropriate recommendations to support the overall goal and not just chuck suggestions out based on the latest technology. Make room for them.

- **Customer services.** Save a couple of seats on the bus for them. They have their fingers on the pulse, they can tell within moments when things go wrong and when they are going right. They will bring a suitcase full of realness with them, but it's worth the extra luggage space.

- **Marketing.** This has long been the 'natural home of the brand' – they are often described as its guardians and managers. You would think that most companies would have worked out that the rise of CX as the main brand driver would have changed all this, but many companies stick to the same old thinking. Marketing need to be on the bus, though, for their branding, consumer and research skills, which they can now apply beyond its traditional application.

- **The Customer.** This may sound a bit trite and obvious, but customers can soon be forgotten, and you cannot take it for granted that they have been considered throughout the whole Delivering process, let alone are central to it. The voice of the customer – and the consumer, for that matter – needs to be heard throughout. They should act as a guide throughout research, and their behaviours and actions evidenced through data. So many companies say they want to 'put the customer first', judging by the early lines in their financial report or on their website, but how many actually deliver it? Not many. Put them on the bus.

- **CEO and MD.** OK, so they might not ride with you on the bus all the time, but if they are not at least at the start and finish of the journey, then it is highly unlikely that a new, compelling CX can be delivered. They need to give it clout, credibility, support, inspiration and drive, and they need to make it clear how the whole programme will be governed so that everyone knows exactly what they are doing and how they will be measured.

Consistent, inspirational messages to both consumers and employees is a critical element of a sustainable brand strategy. Leaders must routinely deliver powerful messages against such questions as, who are we, what do we believe and why do we come to work every day? I.e. the brand.

When this happens, there is a 36% increase in shareholder value.
(The secret sauce of top companies: Aligning your consumer brand and your talent brand; Lippincott, 2013)

Keep the big picture in view

This is often where things go wrong. People are given responsibility for one part of the CX and then concentrate on that part and that part alone, paying no attention to the impact their actions may have on either side. We call this the 'brief over the silo wall' problem, and it is exacerbated when key members of the team are parachuted in at the Delivering stage without knowledge of the big picture.

Our experience tells us that the more people see the whole picture, the more effective they will be, and the hotter the CX.

Seeing the whole picture

In a recent customer-experience mapping session with a long-standing client, the team spotted a single-brand critical process they could make a quick improvement to with very little cost or effort.

So they started working out how to go about it, when a colleague from a different part of the business pointed out that if that process were to change in the way they were suggesting, it would play havoc with the other team's part of the experience. Together, they managed to find a way to avoid the problem – in a way they would not have had they stuck to silo improvement.

This was not the case with a globally famous but long-lost

client of ours that decided to produce its envisioned CX in 'chunks'. We would normally bring everyone together for this session, but the firm insisted on sending people along for 30-minute stints, just to look at their part of the experience. It was silo hell. Nobody left the session knowing what happened either side of their 'chunk', and let's just say that the resulting customer experience is far from seamless, the brand values and tone of voice are inconsistent, and there is a huge amount of waste in the form of inefficiency in the system.

Big picture, big results

Working with a big construction company, we brought our UX team into the whole process. They listened to Exploring debriefs, met a few customers themselves, shared all the thinking behind the vision and attended the innovation sessions. The brutal truth is they didn't contribute much. It wasn't their world, and we thought we may have wasted a lot of time and money. We then asked them to construct the wireframes for six digital experiences that were part of the envisioned CX plan, which was about to go into research. We expected a number of iterations – as is often the case with stimulus, especially with something as complicated as this – but they came back right first time. Perfect! They'd nailed it. We were stunned – this never happens with stimulus. The reason, they explained, was they totally understood the role of the app, the customers who would use it and, crucially, how it fits in with the physical world. It was a lesson we learnt very early on. The apps are now in production.

2. Hot CX busts silos by bringing a company together around one goal

We often wonder how many projects fail due to business silos. In some companies, it's wall-to-wall silos. Departments don't trust each other, insult one another or simply don't want to work together.

You only have to look at the 'conflict' between Operations and Marketing to realise this is the case.

Name-calling

Operators sometimes see Marketers as fluffy, competent only at 'colouring in'. Marketers sometimes see Operators as doers, competent only. Operators accuse Marketers of not living in the real world. Marketers accuse Operators of 'not understanding the customer or the brand'. None of it is true, is it? Marketers aren't fluffy and Operators aren't meatheads, but the barriers exist and they get in the way.

Hot CX cannot be delivered if a business is heavily siloed. Hot CX has a wonderful impact on companies: people stop looking at their jobs from a defensive, personal or departmental perspective to a broader, more customer-oriented one. They can see that what they do influences both the business and the positive outcomes for customers. It's great to see, and it can sometimes change not only the lives of customers but also those who deliver the CX, as they see the impact they are having and enjoy more rewarding cross-functional working relationships.

Hot CX harmony

We had a very complicated and emotionally charged task to help a company develop new customer journeys in the house-rental market. We needed to create CX for different kinds of renters, many of whom were vulnerable and needed help from Social Services, the NHS and other support functions. You can imagine the complexity and emotion involved. This was less of a job and more of a mission.

Both our client's team and our own comprised digital and physical CX specialists, and resulted in one of the most satisfying, efficient and effective projects we have been involved with. All in all, around 200 people were brought together by the project, but the result is a completely seamless and aligned customer experience across all the journeys.

The key to success was that both the physical and digital teams understood what they were doing and why they were doing it. They could see the whole picture and were able to put themselves in the shoes of vulnerable people (which we did by using a huge amount of research stimulus and film). A fantastic by-product of the process was that many people met for the first time and were able to share experiences, problems and solutions; they even made friends as a result. By the end of the project, it was difficult to tell who specialised in what.

3. Build a blueprint for Delivering

Many initiatives, regardless of what they are, fizzle out when there is no delivering or business plan for what they are delivering. Office drawers are full with great ideas that went nowhere. This makes the Realist weep.

Hot CX is real, and essential to its delivery is a proper plan of action. We call it the Delivery Blueprint, but whatever you call it, it should cover what needs to be done, timeframes, responsibilities, measurement criteria, clear prioritisation, and should be built by those who will be responsible for delivering it. Done properly, a Delivery Blueprint that is managed well can power the business towards Hot CX and deliver the ambitions of the senior team and the colleagues who will have to deliver it. Without it, the business can very quickly go off-piste and lose the traction of the programme. It is, if you like, a contract between the senior execs and the rest of the business that links where it is going with what everyone needs to do.

4. Prioritise prioritisation

While the Delivery Blueprint will have priorities embedded within it, prioritisation is such an important part of Hot CX Delivery that it merits a section of its own. We have seen Blueprints without prioritisation, and they are scarily daunting. In this situation, it is likely that companies will be put off from even starting, or they will try to do everything at once, resulting in strangling their own organisation by overloading and through confusion. As the Realist says, 'You can't eat an elephant in one sitting.'

Prioritise for success

Prioritisation is so important that it usually requires an event in its own right to agree it. If you assemble everyone on the bus to debate and decide the basic order of delivery, you can get all the arguments over at once, in the open and in the context of the big picture. This will save time and money in the long run and ensure that the customer, business effort and impact on the business remain central to the plan.

The task of relaunching an old but famous retail brand that had slipped to number two in its market when it had historically been number one was a big project for us to be involved with. In order for its investors to realise its value, the brand had to get back to number one, which required a wholesale look at its customer experience. We had a new vision for the brand, and 88 brand basics were developed around the CX and UX. The only way to get this down to a manageable number was to hold a two-day prioritisation and planning session. It was two days well spent.

Everyone, including the top of the company and CEO, turned up and joined in. The basics were clustered, and plans – including timescales, responsibilities and budget – were produced for 24 basics. Over the next two years, many were implemented, and the company returned to number one. It was then sold successfully in 2016, one year after the session.

Prioritisation should involve an assessment of the influence that each CX initiative will have on the high-level business KPIs and the complexity of delivering it. If an initiative is easy to deliver, with a high impact on the business KPIs, then technically this is described as a 'no brainer'. Just get on with it. If, on the other hand, it has high impact but would prove to be more difficult, then it can be prioritized accordingly after a more detailed business plan is produced. If it is low impact and is very difficult, just don't do it.

Mapping priorities using simple mapping techniques like this help the team see the whole picture of the task before them. This provokes discussion and the sharing of ideas, plus the frequent realisation that new initiatives could fit into existing projects and work streams, thereby avoiding duplication and initiative overload (a Realist's nightmare).

Live mapping can take a mass of initiatives and build a priority map that tests their strategic impact against level of difficulty or cost to deliver.

You can do this using special software, but it isn't as good as Post-its, brown paper and sticky tape, which is more interactive, flexible, visible and real. It's also the Hot CX way.

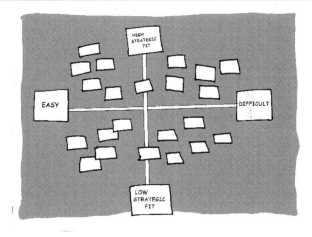

The team will also identify current projects that do not align with the business's overall objectives, and these can be stopped to save resources and avoid damage. Finally, there will be the need to start new projects and pilots that require special project-management skills. The pilots should be set up with the principle of 'fail fast, learn quickly' to ensure there are no delays to the process as a whole.

Ultimately, the output from the priority-mapping process will give the senior management team confidence that the Delivering process is balancing the needs of the customer with those of the business.

Pop-up projects

As the CX programme gathers steam, projects will naturally emerge that require a specialist project team. These can be taken out of the overall CX Delivering Blueprint for speed and efficiency, but care must be taken that they stay aligned and don't become re-siloed. Here are a few examples:

One voice. Any changes to the brand vision will have implications for communications, both internally and externally. This covers everything from posters to social media, TV ads to colleagues' communications, A-boards to websites. The values, personality and tone of voice need to be consistent in digital and physical media or the brand will become confused and people will not know what to expect.

Launch-programme design. The launch of the CX will naturally require a programme to inform and galvanise the company. This should include a narrative and full visualisation at the top level of all physical and digital initiatives, so that colleagues understand and are enthused by the envisioned future.

Brand plumbing. You may discover a few leaks to the CX that need some emergency plumbing. Whether digital or physical, it pays to get them fixed using all the established digital and process-improvement techniques available. This is one you can move fast on, especially when the problems are related to parts of the CX that are brand independent (which is to say that they are functional and do not influence the brand one bit). You might go back and align them later, but in the short term there is no need to wait, especially when leaving them could be dangerous.

Customer-journey mapping. Even though the omnichannel CX will be made up of many customer journeys, there may be outlying journeys that are so specific that a different team of people is required to plot and populate the stages. In this instance, just get the team responsible together – do it, fix any issues and grab any opportunities.

5. Plan in early wins
The no-brainer quick wins you have prioritised have both a business and communication role to perform – they will have an immediate impact on the business and can be relayed to the rest of the team to show progress and gather momentum.

To begin aligning and improving your CX, you should firstly focus on the quick wins. These are the CX pain-points that you know need improving and aligning, but require the least amount of work. They are things you can do right now.

The following turned out to be one of the quickest turnarounds we have ever seen – change happened from day one.

The day after a Visioning session for a family brand based in the south of England, the GM immediately changed the paint colours for the routine maintenance that was due to start the following week to align with the new vision. People could immediately see that the business was serious about a complete change of direction. He followed this at a new CX launch conference by highlighting four initiatives that had already happened, so that momentum was already behind the new strategy. You could hear pennies dropping all around the venue.

6. Put some pilots in place

Wouldn't life be easier if everything was a quick win? The Realist knows that not all CX problems can be fixed overnight. Some, if not many, of your CX issues will be more complex, with cross-functional touch points. If not managed properly, any changes could negatively impact your poor colleagues, making it even worse for the customer.

You don't want to try solving every one of these CX problems your organisation has at the same time: you'll run out of time, resources and motivation, killing any chance of success. Meanwhile, your people and your customers are not going to wait years for you to improve. To manage this, you should run a pilot, using proven improvement tools and techniques.

Pilots are real – well, as real as you can get in the Delivering phase. You can test out opportunities in a controlled fashion, where the business can see the reaction of both customers and colleagues alike. If it works, you can roll it out confidently; if it doesn't, then the risk has been contained and no long-term damage will have been done.

Let's give you an example of a pilot. Imagine you're the head of airport security managing 10 security lanes. Your customers have been complaining how slow and long your security checks are, and you have the data to back this up. Don't just pull some random solutions out of the air and apply them to all 10 lanes. This could go horribly wrong, making things much worse. Instead, focus on one security lane and run a pilot on that lane. This way, you can test your pilot without much disruption to the entire area. Once you've concluded your pilot is a success using data, you can then roll it out to the other nine lanes.

By doing pilots, you're increasing your chances of success. Internally, you'll have a set of results that can be used as evidence and motivation to drive further alignment and improvement work. It'll flush out dissenters and act as a magnet for the 'believers'. Externally, your customers will already be experiencing the improvements. It's a win-win situation.

This is a great opportunity – not only to get the flywheel turning (Jim Collins again!) and show the people of the business that the talking has stopped and the doing has started, it also starts to prove the potential returns from the programme throughout the business.

7. Recognise the business reality

Throughout the whole approach, it is important to achieve a balance between the needs of the customer and those of the business. If this balance is not achieved, then the programme will fail fast. The reality is that there are some things that might be great for the customer, but the cost cannot be justified.

This brings us to the obvious but important point about Hot CX that we first made in the introduction, but it's worth reiterating here. Hot CX does not mean producing the greatest ever, most mind-blowing customer experience that wins endless awards. It means using the brand to drive a compelling omnichannel customer experience that drives business successes. That last bit is the key in this context, as Hot CX is not an end in its own right; it has to drive the success that you have targeted at the start, however you measure it. Financial failure is definitely not hot.

8. Recognise that the basics are often all you need

The encouraging observation for teams starting out on the Delivering stage of the process is that they will be responsible for delivering significant competitive advantage for their business and brand.

It is a sorry state, but in most sectors it is true to say that if the only thing your team delivers are the brand basics, then you will be ahead of the competition. Often, it is all the customer really wants – the feeling is something like, 'make it easy for me, fit in with my life and don't overcomplicate it'.

Brutal about basics

With a bit of help, most companies can be extremely innovative. The number of Brand Amplifiers we develop per company during the Alignment phase is around 50. These are then prioritised down to around 15 and then researched.

Following this part of the process is a moment of brutal realism. Of the 15 we test, half are usually seen as a basic, a no-brainer; a 'why aren't you doing that anyway?' It's always a sobering moment.

The brutal truth is that customers do not spend their waking hours thinking about your brand, unlike you and your teams (hopefully). So getting the basics right can have a big and unexpected effect very quickly. Then you will be allowed to create the Brand Amplifiers and they will appreciate them all the more. Do it the other way round and you will just end up falling from a greater height.

9. Align your Hot CX with your Hot EX
Here is a new, or new-ish, term to grapple with – no groaning at the back, please.

We already have CX and UX as part of the lexicon, so watch out for EX joining at some point soon (if it hasn't already). EX is the new term for Employee Experience. It could have been TX for Team Experience, which is not the language of the Realist, or maybe Colleague Experience, which, of course, is just confusing. So EX it is.

A compelling, even differentiating EX can help the whole process, but it is critical at the Delivering stage. Changing the EX can be a huge signal of change at the start of the process, but its main importance is that it inspires the team to engage with the CX in a greater way and deliver it to a more aligned level, day in, day out.

The evidence that the EX really matters is overwhelming and the subject of much academic effort. But, let's face it: the Realist knows that it's true; they don't need data. It's common sense and they can see it every day.

Some people points

Why people matter:

- Engaged employees are much more productive: engaged employees take an average of 2.69 sick days per year. Disengaged employees take 6.19 sick days per year. (CBI/AXA, 2007 cited in Anderton and Bevan, 2014)

- Companies with high and sustainable levels of engagement through the brand they work for had an average operating margin three times higher than those with lower engagement levels. (Towers Watson, 2012)

- Organisations with engagement levels of 65% or more had shareholder return 22% above the average. Those with engagement levels of 45% or less had shareholder return of 28% below the average. (Aon Hewitt, 2011)

- Employees with high engagement report 28% workplace stress versus 39% with lower engagement. (Aon Hewitt, 2012)

- 70% of engaged employees have a good understanding of customer needs compared with 17% of disengaged employees. (Right Management, 2006)

- 67% of engaged employees are happy to act as advocates for their organisation compared with 3% of disengaged employees. (Gallup, 2003)

- When done effectively, an embedded brand creates a distinctive employee experience that turns your employees into fans, therefore creating a distinctive customer experience. (Harvard Business Review, 2016)

- Robust studies by Harvard have constantly proved the relationship. Here is one study we often refer to: when a business has a vision aligned throughout, there is an increase in productivity of 18% and a reduction in absenteeism of 37%. (Gallup, 2013)

The facts prove how much the EX matters, but even the stellar numbers underplay its importance and potential. One of the underlying reasons it is so important is that employees have more at stake than customers. A customer can drop a brand and move to another if they are not satisfied. Changing jobs, on the other hand, takes a lot more emotional and rational effort, so employees either put up with the status quo or become full-scale detractors. This is a massive lost opportunity, because the same person could be invigorated to help you build the brand you want.

Forgetting your EX

One major retailer was famously fighting new competitors that were disrupting their market and stealing share. Understandably, the retailer lost sight of their own vision, as they were too busy fighting in the trenches with the new competition. The result was that their EX, which had been a major priority and something that made them special, dropped to such an extent that, despite the perks their staff received, even they started shopping with the competitors.

Indeed, for some employees the whole process is a route to improving their lives, and their stories become the stuff of legend internally. You will be amazed by the number of people in your team who appear to be reinvigorated by this process, because they see things happening. They are not just listening to the rhetoric of senior management: they are part of the proof of transformation and the securing of their own futures.

There is another reason that the EX is so key – the undeniable truth that 'the insides leak out'. This is mainly driven by social media, but is accentuated by the press and the sheer openness of society today. This means that while a brand may want to present one face to customers through its CX, it cannot be two-faced and present an entirely different one internally. There is no way it can maintain a situation where the insides of a company are completely at odds with the external projection to its customers.

If you recall the quote from Michael Eisner earlier in the book – the one about a brand being painted in a pointillist style – this is another place where it really comes to life. Your people can either be brand builders or destroyers, depending on how engaged and inspired they are to help you deliver the blueprint.

Are we still on track?

Cross-functional cooperation, unreasonable customers, ferocious competitors, a push for innovation... what could possibly go wrong? Apart from not heeding the lessons of the Critical Success Factors, there are other things that can undermine progress, and we have pooled our experience to identify issues that can cause the CX to go off track.

1. **Losing sight of the customer.** When operational pragmatism starts kicking in, the customer can soon be forgotten. Keep a healthy balance but keep the customer central at all times, and don't get into a situation where you start designing the CX to suit yourself rather than them.

Keep the customer close

Through talking to the CX director of a global financial company, we learnt that the disconnection of some silos from the customer experience was causing problems. In an analysis of the customer transactional data, it was found that 80% of customer complaints were generated by a department that represented 20% of the business's people. No one in that 20% felt in any way connected to the customer, as they had no direct contact with them. This was a remarkable finding, and one that was resolved: complaints fell dramatically, while customer retention increased.

---

2. **Losing sight of the brand.** If all you do is improve the CX, then it is not Hot. It could be good, but not compelling. The brand needs to be the lens through which improvement happens, so it must be present at each and every step of the journey.

3. **Being a purist.** Purity is not a Realist's word. The purist makes everything perfect, logical and elegant. The Realist's world is not like that – it's full of changing priorities, unreasonableness and madness. Doing everything in a nice, measured way may not be a luxury you can afford, and the Realist will have to employ 'fast-fix thinking', sprinting and agile

improvement techniques for both the digital and physical parts of the CX.

4. **Not removing blockers.** It's common for projects to hit obstacles. Therefore, it's essential that there is a method for removing such hurdles. This may require support from senior management, which reinforces the importance of the role they play in change programmes.

5. **Not celebrating the battles that win the war.** Large-scale change programmes may take several years to be fully completed. People will lose energy and confidence over this time, so it's important to celebrate and demonstrate the successes along the way in order to keep the momentum going.

6. **Not making changes stick.** Making change is the easy part – making it stick is difficult. Once improvements are in place, they must be measured, monitored, standardised and constantly checked against the brand, otherwise there is the risk that people will revert to the old ways of working.

7. **Valuing tools over people.** It's common for people who are new to implementing process change to focus on the tools and not the people delivering them.

8. **Lack of urgency.** People will keep putting it off if there is no burning reason to do it. Therefore, it is essential to let everyone know why the CX is important and how it is the battleground for business.

"If you stand still, there is always someone in the market who will bring something new. When things start to soften, it means we are not changing quickly enough."
PAUL POMROY, CEO, McDonald's

9. **Lack of senior-management support.** CX change programmes need senior support to make them happen. Those at the top need to get behind what is happening and why, and need to be seen to be doing so.

10. **Not linking the CX work back to the value it delivers to the business.** By not doing this, the CX could become a silo in its own right. Its performance should always be linked back to the four or five high-level KPIs that the business uses to plot its progress towards achieving its ambition.

A few extra tips for making CX transformation work

- Do a thorough root-cause analysis of any problems you find
- Document the journey to learn lessons
- Start small, learn, adapt, continue and prioritise
- Treat time as invested time, not spent time
- Go to the 'jungle' – go and see things happening for yourself
- Involve people outside your team who have specialist knowledge
- Don't make decisions without supporting data
- Recognise people's efforts

Decide on the level of support

Some companies embark on the process without outside help – they have the skills and resources to make it work themselves. More often than not, though, companies seek the help of specialists, who bring a skill set broadened and honed from experiences in many different sectors and companies. Of course, some companies cannot afford to bring in outside help; they have no choice but to do it themselves, and some need to augment their team as they have only a couple of overworked technicians.

In our experience, the Delivering team will decide between three different levels of support:

1. Periodic review and analysis that brings some engaged outside objectivity to the discussion.
2. Acquiring new skills through training.
3. Outsourced support brought in to help the team deliver and is a supplement to the team for a set time period.

Pumping up the people

Using the brand to drive omnichannel, compelling Customer Experience requires specialist skills in digital development, process improvement, innovation, market research, customer service, journey mapping, business analysis and visioning. Put these skills on the bus, implement the 'dos' (as opposed to the don'ts), avoid the pitfalls, and the next stop for your bus is Hot omnichannel CX and business success. Hurrah! What will almost certainly guarantee you reaching that destination is taking your colleagues with you.

While we have already covered the importance of silo busting, keeping HR on the bus, engagement and involvement, these points are so important that they warrant their own section here. Because it is a particularly big elephant, we have broken it down into five parts and provided some examples to bring them to life.

1. **Employee voice**. Encourage staff to feed back, give them a structure that allows them to do it and ensure they're listened to.

Iceland: employees get to make a difference at work. Every store has an elected member of staff who acts as a link between the shop floor and management, from the store manager to the CEO, on matters big and small – from broken lockers to changing the uniform.

2. **Never-ending narrative.** Provide regular communication about progress towards the vision.

Boots: the company's mission, purpose and values are on display in branches, and the managing director and bosses further down the chain frequently refer to the values in meetings. As a result, staff feel that senior managers truly live the values of the organisation (73%) and that the business is run on a strong set of principles (75%).

Betfred: here, the company's vision and values are everywhere. Team meetings are themed around a different one each week, and they are never forgotten.

3. **Pumped-up managers.** Ensure line mangers understand the brand, are drivers of it on a day-to-day basis and are rewarded for doing so.

Pets at Home: the company hosts 'daily shoals' (morning team meetings), covering everything from sales figures to customer feedback. These serve to ensure that everyone is clear about what is expected of them at work (81%).

Asda: the firm's training and development programmes help its colleagues and managers grow to meet various business challenges. Around 80% of Asda managers begin their careers in store, and the company uses both on-the-job and off-the-job training to develop colleagues at all levels.

Live-it leadership
Ensure leaders don't just repeat the strategy verbatim: they must believe it and live it. Behaving in the tone and style of the brand must come from the very top.

At one client, a seismic shift in culture was required to open the brand up, make it more successful and less stuffy. The new MD walked in on his first day and took his door off its hinges so that people could see him and meet him easily. He also made a big strategic presentation in fancy dress to illustrate that 'having fun' was now a brand value. OK, a bit extreme – but no one was in any doubt about what was required.

4. **Aligned structures and functions.** Have practical, aligned structures to deliver the CX on brand every day. This means the whole employee journey needs to be aligned to the new CX, including recruitment, induction, personal development, day-to-day delivery, reward and recognition, landmarks and leaving.

I'm lovin' it

McDonald's has had to address its entire Customer Experience – from food sourcing to service – in order to arrest the decline suffered by the company in the early 2000s. The publicity surrounding the salt, sugar and fat content of its meals drew added unwanted attention to its estate of ugly, dated restaurants, and the whole proposition seemed to have had its day. It could so easily have become what we call a 'Yesterbrand'.

Under Paul Pomroy, McDonald's has been looking at its entire CX and overhauling all 1,257 restaurants. The décor is being upgraded, digital ordering kiosks are being installed, table service is being offered, and iPads are being provided to keep kids entertained. There has also has been an investment in kitchens, so that food can be prepared as soon as an order is placed, rather than batch-cooking burgers and keeping them warm. The company is now sourcing only 100% British beef and potatoes, and proudly promotes its sustainable-sourcing policy and support for grass-roots football. The chain even has a nutrition calculator, which allows you to work out the levels of salt, sugar and fat in your food – as much a statement of confidence than anything else. The whole proposition is heading towards alignment and is going beyond whether the interaction is digital or physical and into the whole way the business operates.

Love 'em or hate 'em, you have to say that they are getting towards Hot CX. I go in every now and again for a coffee (pretty good, I have to admit), just to see how Hot they are getting. It's pretty impressive.

Delivering summary

My dad may be old school, but he now knows what we do for a living. We help make customer experiences – compelling ones that are driven by the brand and deliver business success.

Delivering is the most satisfying stage of CX development. It's when all the hard work comes to life and customers start experiencing what you have done and telling people about it. When the results start materialising in terms of revenue, better sentiment, share value and a happier and rewarded team in the board room and at the frontline, there really is nothing better. It's what we get out of bed to do.

Hot CX Delivering turns strategy into actual experience in both digital and physical worlds, which in turn becomes the strongest and most sustainable communication medium that you will ever have. It also busts silos and develops strong bonds inside and outside the business. And it puts a smile on your face.

Delivering: what's hot and what's not

Hot	Not
Getting the right people on the bus	Losing sight of the customer
Keeping the big picture in sight	Losing sight of the brand
Going silo bustin' and engaging people and teams	Being a purist
Building a Blueprint for delivery	Letting the blockers block
Prioritising prioritisation (don't try to eat an elephant in one sitting)	Not celebrating battles won
Planning in early wins	Letting change become unstuck
Putting some pilots in place	Valuing tools over philosophy
Recognising the business reality	Lacking urgency
Recognising that, often, the basics are all you need	Trying to do this without visible senior-management support
Aligning your Hot CX to your Hot EX	Forgetting to link the benefits to its value to the business

5. MEASURING

"You can have data without information, but you cannot have information without data."
DANIEL KEYS MORAN

Making CX measurement work

Many years ago, I was verbally attacked in a meeting by a management consultant when I suggested, 'If it doesn't get measured, it doesn't get done.' I thought I was being clever, but he tore into me with such a volley of venomous language and accusations of 'naivety' that he left me stunned – mainly because my assailant had forgotten that he had said the exact same words in a meeting only six months earlier.

On reflection, and with the benefit of experience, I don't think the comment was right. If you follow the logic and believe that thousands of gestures build a brand, it would mean that there is a need for a correspondingly high number of measures. This smacks of over-measurement, which can suffocate a business and slow things down dramatically. But, by the same token, CX Realists know that you can't skimp on measurement – that would be madness – and that the right measures taken at the right time enable companies to monitor progress so that resources can be applied and withdrawn efficiently and effectively and tactical changes made to keep the strategy on track.

This, of course, doesn't sound too tricky, but there are a number of barriers that nearly always get in the way.

- The responsibility for the data you need mostly resides in different departments: IT, Marketing, Operations, Sales, Finance and HR. Nobody bothers sharing and people are defensive about their own data.

- The data from the different methods is collected differently at different times using different methods, so comparisons are nigh on impossible.

- Many measurements include a mad mix of 'clever' indices that have no connection to each other or are not understood across the business.

- Tracking is stuck in old-era thinking and includes only traditional brand measures such as 'awareness'.

- The data is too historical to be of any use, or measures things that can't be fixed.

So a new approach and a new attitude are required. The approach is one that aligns CS measures to the top business metrics, has clearly defined and separate strategic and tactical roles, mixes hard business data with consumer-tracking data, takes measures inside the business as well as outside, has an easy-to-understand methodology and is predictive. The attitude is one of shared responsibility and trust, of using data as a guide to help you judge what is happening, and treating numbers with respect and caution.

If you successfully build a measurement toolkit and surround it with the right attitude, the upside is huge. You can predict behaviour, pre-empt problems, align resources, maintain differentiation, remain sustainably compelling and bust silos. In short, you will galvanise the business.

Hot numbers and where to find them – building a measurement toolkit

Let's not forget that Hot CX equals great business, so developing a toolkit to measure progress is business-critical. We have seen all sorts of measurement strategies used by our clients, and believe that the numbers can be divided into two different types.

1. **Hard business data:** facts that show what has happened and is happening in the business.

2. **Tracking research:** a programme of concise, intelligent conversations with customers, consumers and colleagues.

Let's look at the two types of measurement in more detail.

1. HARD BUSINESS DATA

Hard data can be operational or efficiency measures such as the number of visits to a website, traffic at a help desk and visits to a store, or they can be customer metrics such as retention and conversion rates.

Much of this data already exists. Let's face it, most companies are more data rich than they realise, and their use of this information varies alarmingly. This is surprising given that there is a strong correlation between high-performing organisations and those who see data as a major asset. Hot numbers = hot business.

Here are some other hard-data measures that should form part of your Hot CX measuring toolkit. Let's start with three purely digital ones:

1. Visitor intent and task completion

Customers normally set out with a task and goal in mind when they engage digitally, and only they can provide feedback in the context of their intentions or tell us if they were ultimately satisfied with the digital interaction and whether or not they could complete what they set out to do.

So listening to what they say about the experience and monitoring the level of task completions have become key customer-experience metrics and have opened up a whole new world of measurement using digital analytics. So use these numbers to understand how your customers are feeling, thinking and behaving.

2. Abandonment rates

Once you have spent time and money getting people to your site, the last thing you want is to lose them. According to the Baymard Institute, the average shopping basket abandonment rate is 68.53%. Permit me a 'wow!' here and a moment's contemplation. Let's get that straight: only a third of people who have decided to buy something online actually make that purchase. That's a terrible waste.

Removing barriers to purchase – such as hidden fees, expensive shipping options and inconvenient payment methods – represent some of the answers; making everything frictionless and easy are others, so watch those numbers and be prepared to remove barriers.

3. Time on site

It is debatable whether this is important or not, but some people like to monitor 'time on site'. Those who think that we tend to stay longer around things we like and find rewarding in some way believe the same is true of websites. The amount of time spent on your site could be an indicator of how fresh and interesting your content is, but the counter-argument is it could be a sign that your website is cumbersome and difficult to use. Many people also argue that you actually want time on site to be kept to a minimum, as it indicates that it is navigable and that task completion is easy.

Another way of monitoring this is by watching what's happening on advisor chats, in particular the topics being covered, which content gets the best content interaction and, of course, the number of times people share your content.

Here are some measures that can be digital and physical:

4. Conversion rate

Following any interaction with a customer, you need to determine the likelihood that they will take some further action. If your customer experience is 'hot', this number will sizzle.

Those companies that have particularly long sales cycles need to design their customer experiences in a way that keeps a prospective customer moving along their individual buyer journey seamlessly and efficiently. Providing the best user experience (both physical and digital) throughout the buying process will help improve the conversion rates from one touchpoint to the next.

The offline/online conversion rate is also important ¬– such as click and collect, book a test drive, book an appointment, call back. So understand the journey and the implications for action of differing rates of conversion between the different stages.

5. Retention rate

Once a prospective customer has made their first purchase, they represent a major opportunity for any organisation. Increasing retention rates has obvious revenue opportunities, and it has been proven time and time again that Hot organisations providing Hot CX have demonstrably lower customer churn rates. So monitor yours closely and take corrective action if it starts moving in the wrong direction.

6.   Acquisition rate

We nearly always need new customers – you don't need us to tell you that they are essential for long-term growth. Giving customers a better experience from first point of contact keeps them engaged throughout the buyer journey and makes them more likely to make a purchase. Higher acquisition rates correlate directly with higher rates of income. So knowing what proportion of your customers in any given period are first-time visitors – or, more importantly, purchasers – will be a huge indicator of future performance.

7.   Resolved issues

Looking at all the issues that your customer-service team has solved forms a snapshot of your company's customer service. Regardless of how successful your company is, there will always be some problems and grievances. However, if you have a team that can solve them efficiently, the benefits in extra sales and extra loyalty are well documented. So set your standard of efficient response time and measure against it, but make sure it is realistic and helps motivate the staff resolving the problems.

8.   Repeat visits

Being able to measure both the frequency and regularity of repeat visits will provide evidence of how well the site satisfies customer needs. Make sure, then, that you capture data to measure and differentiate between the first or second timers, the frequent and regular, the less frequent but regular, and the infrequent.

And one that is an overall customer measure.

9. Customer lifetime value (CLV)

The net value of revenue flows from each customer.

10. Benchmarking

Less a hot number and more a hot principle, but it is nearly always worthwhile knowing how your company is doing in comparison to your competitors. Your customers are likely to be their customers as well, and even loyal customers may choose one of your competitors for a single purchase, or at least see what they have to offer.

As well as measuring these things against benchmarks, it is also important to look at trends over time more than individual stats and whether they are good or bad versus the benchmarks. Progress matters more than snapshots.

2. TRACKING RESEARCH
Putting hard data in its place
'Hard data.' The term alone makes us puff out our chests and feel tough. 'With hard data we can take on the world!' Well, you can take it on, but you will not win. Hard data is great because you can't easily argue with it, but to rely on it totally is neither Hot CX nor customer-experience realism.

Hard data helps you see what is happening, or, if you like, the hard output of all your work. Historical hard data should also be the bedrock of prediction, against which targets should be set and monitored. But hard data cannot do everything; there will be gaps in the measurement toolkit that, if left unfilled, can leave you dangerously exposed. But it is easy to put right. Tracking research can complete your toolkit, but you need the right kind of tracking.

Why tracking needs to change
Let's address two big and current issues in measurement.

1. The limitations of Net Promoter Score (NPS)

When we begin to talk about measurement with CX professionals, NPS is nearly always the first thing that is mentioned. In fact, it is often the only thing that is mentioned. This should be alarming to any CX Realist and Hot CX practitioner, but part of the reason for this is that Fred Reichheld claimed, in his 2003 Harvard Business Review article, that NPS is 'The One Number You Need to Grow'. We argue that while it offers a simplistic measure that can be benchmarked and has proven to correlate with business success, it does not provide the data required to help you work out what progress you are making towards the vision, what is and isn't working, and why.

'NPS has some well-known limitations, including its difficulty to understand the absolute economic value of the score (NPS is a relatively weak indicator of actual purchase behaviour), and the fact that NPS won't reveal why a score is low, high or in between.' (Gartner, 2015)

2. Old-era CX tracking is a mess of different techniques and methodologies that reinforce silos, cause confusion, often get ignored and do not give one big picture.

If we believe, and most people do, that brands are built by the thousands of touchpoints in the customer experience (by which we mean physical and digital), it follows that a number of existing tracking programmes, or at least elements of them, can be combined to create one consolidated measurement tool. It's what the Realist would do.

The four we have in mind are brand tracking, customer satisfaction, employee satisfaction and advertising tracking. They are usually separate programmes administered differently, using different questions in different formats and with different owners. Far better to work out what you really need and, with a bit of skill and the right attitude, you can combine all the essentials in one CX tracking programme.

The programme should also recognise that some tracking is strategic and requires longer, more detailed methodology, while some is tactical and needs frequent feedback, often on a real-time basis. This regularly gets mixed up, and questions are asked in real time that cannot be actioned in real time. This is a waste. So it's worth being very clear about the objectives of each element of the programme to achieve the balance of real-time tactical and strategic feedback. If this is all wrapped up in one programme, it will inevitably save time and cut costs, bust silos, galvanise the business and cut waste.

Developing tracking for the new era

This sounds like an apocryphal story, but it is true.

We had just attended with our client a 150-slide debrief from one of the world's leading brand-tracking agencies. All very pleasant. Great croissants. It lasted nearly four hours and there were four very nice presenters. We were shown all sorts of indices, unique measures and a 'critical relationship analysis'. It was all very, very clever but, as we left, our client tapped me on the shoulder and said, 'That's all very good, but have we done well or badly?' She was obviously a CX Realist.

This got us thinking: if a very experienced and respected marketer can't work out from the numbers whether things are going well or badly (neither did we, by the way – we had to work it out on the train back home), then what chance do those responsible for operations, human resources, customer service and all the other elements of the business that are delivering the brand through the customer experience have? It is much easier to ignore the data, put the report on a shelf to gather dust and carry on regardless. What a terrible, terrible waste.

Two days later, we received another call from a client. He was the marketing director of a national retailer and he happily informed us that they had engaged another company to measure the effectiveness of the brand-led CX programme we had developed with them, as we didn't have a product to do it. He thought I would be delighted. He was wrong. It was time for action – we needed to address the problem.

So here is where we unashamedly talk about a product we have invented. We have thought about ways of writing about it in a less 'selling' way, but couldn't do it, despite a number of attempts. We invented this because it was needed; it really isn't rocket science, but it does address all the issues our clients were encountering. Please forgive us.

Let's go BAMing.

The Brand Alignment Monitor™ (BAM)

It was plain to us that while customers and clients had moved on significantly, tracking had not. Most people agree that we have entered a new era of brand building and that we now need a new way to track progress that aligns with the ways that brands are now built (through the CX/UX) – or, in other words, the thousands of small touchpoints. It also had to align with the other needs of our times: value, a direct link to action and brutal clarity.

So we got to work on a new product. We worked with people who had very big brains to make sure it was rooted in sound, robust science. But after all the maths and analysis, we decided that all we really needed was to put our Realist's hat on – some common sense and CX experience.

We call it the Brand Alignment Monitor, which of course gives it a mildly entertaining acronym that provided us with a lot of infantile fun at the beginning – especially when we found out it was also a brand of condoms. The BAM measures the things that need measuring, does it using one simple metric that everyone can understand, tells you what is working, what isn't working and why, and, because of its simplicity, helps busts silos. It has proved to be a great help on the road to Hot CX, and is so simple and easy to use that you can do it yourselves – you don't need us to work it out for you.

Putting the BAM together

The sample and the importance of 'inside out'

The first question is this: among which group do you want to know how well the vision is being delivered? The most common answer to this is a brand's customers and potential customers. We added a third audience – colleagues. Our reasoning was this: if brands are built from the 'inside out', it stands to reason that your own teams know before anyone else what is happening to your CX and brand. This was less of an assumption and more of a fact, as 20 years of tracking reveals that the internal team knows at least six months before the impacts of a poor CX hits the tills.

Murder on the high street

In the mid-1990s, before we left JWT, we were running a very basic tracker for a competitor of Marks & Spencer. M&S at the time was the darling of the high street; there was never any thought that it might be heading for a fall – and, of course, the company had no idea there was anything wrong, as it famously didn't carry out any research.

Every month, we would gather around our PCs and watch a quite remarkable change occurring. Point by point, touchpoint by touchpoint, M&S was destroying its business. We had a cell of M&S shoppers and staff in the sample, and basic tracking measures against value for money, understanding customers, service and value were all heading, very slowly but consistently, downwards. All we used was a score out of 10, but the trend was established six months before the impact was felt at the tills and recognised in the boardroom and City. It is argued that M&S has never fully recovered.

It's amazing to think that all M&S had to do was regularly ask a sample of customers, potential customers and colleagues to mark the elements of the Customer Experience out of 10, and all that pain might have been avoided.

Murder in a conference

In late 2012, we presented the results of the first BAM to the Financial Services Conference in London. We had based the survey on financial-services brands as they were in the media limelight, and although we expected some interesting and entertaining results, we did not expect them to be quite as revealing as they proved to be.

The BAM told us that the Co-op was the best of a bad bunch, and the overall alignment of its delivery to its vision as an ethical bank was better than any other bank. The problem, however, was that the sample of bank workers in the survey gave the Co-op brutally low marks for alignment with its vision, so we boldly predicted stormy waters ahead for the bank. Of course, no one took us seriously, especially the team from the Co-op, who looked like they were about to lamp us. What happened next is now history, but the evidence was all there. As we said earlier: it's not rocket science.

What we need to know

Having sorted the sample, we focused on identifying what we need to know to light the path to Hot CX nirvana. We drew on our experience and talked to clients, and it was easy to break it into three core areas:

1. **The standing of the brand.** We need to know whether customers, potential customers and our colleagues (especially those at the frontline) think the brand is aligned to its vision, values and personality, and the direction in which it is going. We also need to know how this benchmarks against the key competitors in the market.

2. **A diagnosis of what is and isn't working.** Whatever the trajectory of the brand, whether it is going towards the vision or away from it, every company needs to know 'why'. This will be different for each organisation, so the first thing is to establish the critical things the organisation must do to deliver the CX and brand vision, and then measure progress against them. This applies across the physical and digital elements of the CX. They may be the physical welcome, the digital payment process or the look of the advertising. Whatever they are, we need to first identify them and then make sure we ask our customers, potential customers and colleagues what they think of them and whether they are aligned to the vision.

3. **Action.** The CX Realist wants to know what this all means in terms of behaviour, and needs to monitor and predict propensity to purchase or visit, expected levels of frequency and spend, and the impact on recommendation levels.

So, a quick recap: effective new-era CX and brand tracking needs three samples – customers, potential customers and colleagues. It needs to measure progress against the vision, provide a diagnosis across the important aspects of the CX, and then give guidance on the potential impact of all this on behaviour.

The last big part of tracking is 'how to measure'. Or, in other words, what methods and mathematical wizardry are required to provide the indices and measures through which the CX is measured? So how many different methods do you think we need? And how many key indices?

We thought one was enough.

Create one way of measuring so that everyone understands what good looks like
Progress should be measured in a way that is easily understood. If employees across the whole organisation understand what is a good and bad score, they will engage with it and care about it. So if numerous disparate measurement systems are used and understood only by the Marketing department, it is highly unlikely that the data is being used to drive delivery of the brand's vision. In fact, it is nigh on impossible without the same understanding of what good and bad looks like throughout the organisation, such as Operations, Marketing, Human Resources, Customer Services and anywhere else where responsibility for the CX lies.

Given that people are more familiar with the scoring system for NPS than any other methodology (when we last looked, it was used by more than 50% of FTSE companies), that it makes intuitive sense and is proven to correlate with business success, we thought we should use the same basic NPS questioning methodology throughout the tracking programme.

As a quick reminder, this is how it works: customers are asked their level of agreement with the statement 'How likely are you to recommend X to your friends and family?' on a scale of 0 to 10, where 10 is very highly likely and 0 is not. As many of you will know, NPS is a customer-loyalty metric developed by (and a registered trademark of) Fred Reichheld, Bain & Company and Satmetrix Systems, and is used by many companies at specific points in the CX. A score of 60+ is considered world class, and less than 10 is poor. People get used to judging what good looks like, and the scores can be benchmarked.

So for each part of the customer experience (CX and UX), we develop statements and ask customers, potential customers and colleagues their level of agreement with them. This way, scores are always between -100 and +100, so we always know how each part of the CX is performing relative to others and we have a universal understanding of what is good and bad across the whole business. It's as simple as that.

An example of how this can work
To demonstrate how it and the BAM works, we have put together a hypothetical example based on a brand we have made up. It's a theme-park brand, which, for the purposes of this example, we have called Bliss. Let's imagine there are 26 Bliss theme parks across the world; the brand also makes films for TV and has created a number of valuable intellectual properties over time, on which some of its rides are based. It also has a number of shops and we should consider it a major global player. We all want to go to Bliss!

We started by creating a brand vision (positioning and values), and used our experience of the sector to suggest what the key drivers of that vision might be. We then populated it with dummy data. Hopefully, you will see as we take you through the methodology that it is possible to have one method of measurement that everyone can understand, predicts the future and measures CX delivery in a realistic way.

The Bliss brand vision
Positioning: We bring happiness to people of all ages by creating the most magical entertainment in the world. Bliss is the happiest place on earth.

Using some of the techniques discussed earlier in the book, we created three core brand values and described what each does in one sentence.

Value 1: Magical storytelling
We entertain by telling stories, and no one knows how to engage, grip and enthral people of all ages as much as us.

Value 2. Seamlessness
There are no holes in our magic. Once you enter our world, there are no gaps and no leaks – just total escape from the real world.

Value 3. Doing good
We value the good in the world and stand up for what is right and fair. We are committed to making the world a happier place and act as a force for good, wherever we are in the world.

Whether you like the vision and think we have created something compelling or not is really not the point here (though we'd prefer it if you could at least see where we are coming from), it's the technique that's important. Our next step is to take the positioning and values and turn them into simple statements about the brand. In the real world, this is a rigorous process involving those who will use the output – though in this instance, of course, we did it ourselves. We then ask customers, potential customers and colleagues how much they agree with them: 0 = no agreement at all, and 10 = total agreement.

These are the statements we developed:

To test progress on the positioning (Happiest place on earth), we developed these statements:

- Bliss is committed to making people happy
- Bliss stands for happiness
- No company makes people happy as much as Bliss

To test progress on the values, we developed these statements:

Magical storytelling

- At Bliss, you enter magical stories
- Bliss tells stories that grip you

Seamlessness

- Bliss helps you lose yourself in another world
- Bliss makes you forget all your cares

Doing good

- Bliss is a force for good in the world
- Bliss stands for a better world

We then ask the level of agreement to these statements among the three audiences of customers, potential customers and colleagues, and apply the NPS methodology to the results (taking agreement scores of 10 and 9 and subtracting disagreement scores of 6 and below). This allows us to establish the standing of Bliss among its various target audiences. We can track progress over time, benchmark the results against competitors and analyse them by different target typologies, such as 'committed fans' or 'cool kids', or socio demographics such as 14 to 18-year-olds – or whatever has been determined as Bliss's target audience.

For the purposes of this example, we have made the data up, and chart 1 shows how well progress is being made towards the brand vision.

Sample: Current Bliss Customers: agreement with 'the happiest place on earth'. The Net index is calculated by taking the proportion who agreed with this statement at levels of 6 and below away from the proportion who agreed at 9 or 10 out of 10. The proportion who answered 7 or 8 in terms of level of agreement are considered 'ambivalent' and ignored.

	Mar 15	Sep 15	Mar 16	Sep 16	Mar 17	Sep 17	Cool Kids
Net Index	+13	+17	+32	+21	+39	+45	+11

The commentary for this chart would probably go something like this for the audience of Current Bliss Customers: *There has been impressive progress from a low start point in March 2015. By September 2017, Bliss has almost reached 'exceptional' levels of alignment, although customers classified as 'cool kids' do not believe that Bliss is 'the happiest place on earth'.*

This is the first time you have seen this data, so you will not be aware of what good looks like, but just as with NPS, the scale is -100 to +100: scores over 50 are exceptional, between 30 and 49 are good to very good, 10-29 are average. You may also have run the question against a competitor to see if your brand is differentiating itself. Bliss may be scoring +11 among kids as 'The happiest place on earth', but Alton Towers might be getting +50, so you know where your problem might be.

Of course, looking at this purely from a customer's perspective doesn't provide the whole story. The second sample is Potential Customers, which could comprise a sample of competitors' customers and those who are positive to Bliss but have yet to visit. Here is some hypothetical data from this sample:

Sample: Current Competitor Customers: agreement with 'the happiest place on earth'. The Net index is calculated by taking the proportion who agreed with this statement at levels of 6 and below away from the proportion who agreed at 9 or 10 out of 10. The proportion who answered 7 or 8 in terms of level of agreement are considered 'ambivalent' and ignored.

	Mar 15	Sep 15	Mar 16	Sep 16	Mar 17	Sep 17	Cool Kids
Net Index	-23	-16	-8	+2	+15	+23	-32

Bliss executives would be pleased to see that their brand is improving the delivery of its vision. However, it is not strong alignment, and one drag on the brand might be 'cool kids', who do not believe that Bliss is delivering against its vision and are probably negatively influencing others through social media.

The third sample is 'colleagues'. This will be made up from people across the organisation, but many will be working at the frontline. Remember, they are a good predictor of what is going to happen – they know first. Here is some sample data.

Sample: Colleagues: agreement with 'the happiest place on earth'. The Net index is calculated by taking the proportion who agreed with this statement at levels of 6 and below away from the proportion who agreed at 9 or 10 out of 10. The proportion who answered 7 or 8 in terms of level of agreement are considered 'ambivalent' and ignored.

	Mar 15	Sep 15	Mar 16	Sep 16	Mar 17	Sep 17
Overall	+17	+24	+21	+32	+42	+50
Employed in past 5 years	+24	+28	+31	+36	+48	+54
More than 5 years in the job	+9	+15	+6	+7	+11	+13

The future does look good for Bliss, though, as its scores among its colleagues are positive, which is not always the case (many BAMs believe the brand they work for is not delivering it vision). But Bliss may have to apply some resource to colleagues who have been working at Bliss for more than five years, as their scores are much lower than those of new starters.

By using the same technique with Bliss's values, we will begin to reveal more about what is and isn't working. For example, Bliss is doing a lot of work to protect the environment, and the scores against 'doing good' will reveal if this is having an effect or not. As the scoring system is exactly the same throughout, people will get to know very quickly what is good and what needs improving.

Measuring how Bliss is delivering its vision through its touchpoints is a fundamental need, but if it wants to practise Hot CX, the people running the company will want to know more about why the movement is happening so it can take the appropriate action. This is done by measuring agreement with statements about the high-level processes and strategies that have been identified as the drivers of the vision.

For our example, the key processes within the CX/UX for Bliss are (hypothetically):

- Customer-driven products – all products and services are based on customer and consumer needs and desires
- Seamless interfaces – every customer touchpoint works seamlessly and in alignment with the brand
- Passionate people – colleagues are obsessed with service and are committed to Bliss
- Expert communications – our communications are always relevant, targeted and interesting for our customers

Using the same technique as before, we then derive statements that align with the drivers and measure agreement to them to give an effective diagnosis of the situation.

This is how the statements using these key drivers for Bliss might look:

Consumer-driven products
- Bliss feels relevant to me
- Bliss has products I love
- Bliss always has the best deals

Seamless interfaces
- Bliss's website is easy to navigate
- Dealing with Bliss is always easy
- Bliss's automated phone service saves me time and effort
- The Bliss app makes it easy to keep in touch

Passionate people
- Everyone I speak to at Bliss is friendly and helpful
- The people at Bliss are passionate about what they do
- It feels like the people at Bliss really enjoy working there
- The people at Bliss make dealing with the company as easy as possible

Expert communications
- Bliss keeps me up to date in just the right way – not too much, and not too little
- I like the way Bliss speaks to me
- Bliss talks like it's the expert
- The ads I see for Bliss make me want to check it out

The same methodology is used as before. Customers, Potential Customers and Colleagues are asked for their level of agreement with each statement, and scores between -100 and +100 produced. The great thing is that because everyone in Bliss, whether they are in HR, Operations, Marketing or Finance, knows what good looks like, they can identify issues and successes.

The final part of the BAM is the 'Action' section, which covers the key metrics from the list of KPIs that align with your business ambition.

Testimonial from Justin Platt, Managing Director Resort Theme Parks, Merlin Entertainments:

'The BAM has quickly become an important brand-tracking tool within Resort Theme Parks at Merlin. It has taken the best elements of our old brand tracker and added a level of thoroughness, which helps us to make decisions and implement change quickly. All reporting is timely, succinct and insightful, and our key stakeholders find it very easy to interpret and use the data. I'd strongly recommend the BAM.'

So that's the BAM – a new tracking system for a new era. *Stop me and buy one.

Key Performance Indicators for customer experience

Traditionally, customer experience analytics were solely diagnostic in nature, meaning experts analysed what customers do and say about the past to improve their experience in the future. Hot CX requires a balanced programme of hard business measures and tracking – not only to help highlight where things are going wrong and where resource is required, but also to assess progress against the brand vision, highlight what's working and what isn't, identify where to amplify the brand, monitor the levels of differentiation and work out how compelling the proposition is.

The programme needs to be robust, help companies keep their eyes on the horizon and their feet on the ground, be current and predictive, speak to existing and potential customers and ensure that colleagues are involved. It must be easy to understand, actionable, practical, and the measurement programme must be embedded in the business to help inform decisions, and directly impact the business. Only then will your Hot CX be driven by hot numbers.

Measuring: what's hot and what's not

Hot	Not
Creating a baseline of the current situation	Not knowing where you are starting from
Analysing how the CX data directly influences the top business metrics	Collecting data in isolation from the business impact
A mix of regular strategic dips and tactical continuous data	Treating strategy and tactics as the same thing
Mixing hard data with tracking data	Trying to do everything with one method
Not relying on NPS alone	Relying on NPS
Taking measures from inside the business	Ignoring those who know first
Identifying what may be getting in the way of colleagues delivering the CX	Not highlighting issues
Knowing what direction you are going in and why	Not providing the 'why' to the 'what'
Having a simple, single metric	Numerous nonsensical, meaningless indices that no one understands or uses
Sharing the data and reporting back	Keeping all the learning in the hands of a small group of people

Focusing on the wrong thing

One very well-known ex-client of ours was fixated with its in-store service-satisfaction scores. They rejoiced when the monthly scores rose by half a per cent and went into a deep dive of depression when they fell by the same amount. However, the service-satisfaction scores were always in the 90% to 95% range. The client also agonised about why the figures were not 100% and, despite multiple attempts to help them look at other measures or the bigger picture, the fixation remained.

They went bust. All their stores were sold. They were overtaken and became irrelevant.

MEASURING

HOT CX FOR B2B

Gone shipping

Acetates. We had our arms full of them as we crossed Fleet Street in central London, heading very nervously to our first pitch as Brand Vista.

It was 2000, and the credibility and security of being part of one of the biggest and most well-known communications agencies in the world had been shed – there were just the two of us now, and we had a date to talk about something people didn't really know about: brand alignment. As we struggled to keep the rain off the acetates and avoid being run over, the nerves seemed to gather momentum, and we began asking ourselves how it had come to pass that our first pitch was about to be to a company that supplies ship management and related marine services to the global shipping industry. Two ex-Mad Men and a global shipping company? It didn't make sense. You couldn't get more business-to-business than this – it was an industry we knew nothing about, and surely the culture wouldn't fit? How gloriously wrong we were!

Let me get back to the acetates. This was our opener:

> *Brand alignment is a simple but very powerful concept pioneered by Brand Vista. The fundamental premise is that, through customer insight, you are able to develop a brand definition that outlines the position, personality and indeed the promise to the marketplace. Brand alignment occurs when the brand promise is delivered consistently through everything that the company does.*

There it is, in black and white, word for word. Acetate number one. Far too many words for a company's opener, of course – we wouldn't dream of presenting a slide like that nowadays, and we are still squirming looking at some of the phrases. The end sentence grabbed our attention, though: 'Brand alignment occurs when the brand promise is delivered consistently through everything that the company does.' It's a long-winded way of saying, 'Use the brand to drive a compelling omnichannel customer experience.' Language apart, we like to think that we were not too far off where we are today.

We presented our 40 or so very serious acetates to V Ships and, after our initial nervousness had died down, we realised that global shipping companies, brand alignment, B2B and two recently outed Mad Men are actually a very good and natural fit. Luckily, we were offering exactly what they wanted, and what followed was one of the most enjoyable and productive relationships of our first five years. We had chalked our first win. We were up and running.

Apart from enjoying a nostalgic trip down memory lane (acetates? Hard to believe, isn't it?), the point to all this is that although we have talked almost exclusively so far about the relationship between business and consumers, there is no reason to suppose that the same process, methods and principles we have outlined shouldn't be as relevant and effective in developing a compelling CX for businesses who do business with other businesses.

Our first pitch, which still shines so bright in the memory, proves it. Just like in B2C, V Ships has customers who have emotional and rational needs and desires; of course, they are different ones, but nevertheless, these customers are not robots and their emotional levers are there to be pulled. Another difference is that there are fewer of them than in a B2C environment, which simply means that each one is potentially very important, and when we are exploring, as we saw earlier, we need a few different techniques to research customers. V Ships is also a big company and needed a vision it could get behind and then organise itself and its CX (although nobody had heard of CX at the time) around the vision. So the approach we took had to be different to the one we would have taken had V Ships been a cruise-ship brand selling to the general public.

We started by exploring the views of the leadership team to understand the origins of the company and their ambition for it. We interviewed ship owners and some crew, and then we went to the 'jungle' to talk to the shipping press. All this work was then consolidated and used to help guide a new architecture for the brand and a top-line alignment plan. This was all presented on said acetates, which are buried somewhere in my garage. Not much difference there between B2B and B2C, I hope you will agree.

We worked with V Ships for five years, and the company now has 70 offices in 34 countries; it has been successfully bought and sold twice by different private-equity companies and is now owned by Advent International. V Ships now manages more than 1,000 vessels and has a crew roster of 26,000, with over 47,000 people in offshore roles. I hope that gives you an idea of who they are, how big they are and how 'business to business' they are. And that is the point: a compelling omnichannel CX is just as important in B2B – there are just subtle details in the journey to get there that need to change.

Hot CX and B2B

You'll need some reassurance that everything we have to say about delivering Hot CX in business-to-business is not just based on V Ships, though. So the list below shows the other companies we have worked with. The other obvious point here (but still worth stressing) is that we are in a B2B market ourselves. It's our game; it is how we put the dinner on our own plates.

Clients:
- AstraZeneca - Global pharmaceuticals
- AutoProtect - Automotive insurance products to dealers and manufacturers
- Balfour Beatty - Infrastructure construction services
- Bibby Line Group - Global shipping, marine services, logistics, financial services
- Bibby Financial Services - Global financial factoring for SMEs
- BLM - Insurance legal services
- Brookson - Specialist accountancy services and an umbrella employment solution
- Dental Buying Group (DBG) - Dental and doctor practices support, ensuring compliance to consumables
- GB Group - Global data-identity experts
- JSC - Sports sponsorship and public relations
- Navitas - Global pharmacovigilance consulting and business process outsourcing safe, cost-effective, technology-driven clinical trials

- OAG - Global aviation data and consulting
- V Ships - Ship management
- Plexus Cotton - Cotton traders
- Newcastle Gateshead Initiative - Regional investment Initiative
- Blackpool - City council
- The EU Robotics SPARC Initiative - The Partnership for Robotics in Europe

Rather than repeat ourselves here, we thought we would use this chapter to simply highlight what is different about using the brand to develop and deliver a compelling omnichannel CX in a B2B environment, as compared with B2C. Most of the objectives, principles and methods are the same as those in the original sections, so if you are planning to take on this task for a business selling to a business, for some top tips, simply go back and look at it through B2B spectacles.

1. Exploring

Just like in B2C. Terry knows.

"If you do not know where you come from, then you don't know where you are, and if you don't know where you are, then you don't know where you're going. And if you don't know where you're going, you're probably going wrong."
TERRY PRATCHETT, I Shall Wear Midnight

Whether it's B2C or B2B, you need to know your starting place. You cannot set off in the dark and hope to achieve Hot CX.

The three eyes of exploring in B2B
So here's what's different:

The B2B Difference	What to do about it
Fewer customers (and consumers)	Is it possible, or necessary, to do both quantitative and qualitative research? If your customer audience is 150 or more you can do both, but the quantitative sample can be significantly less and still robust because it will be a high percentage of the universe.
Respondents have less time	Using telephone and Skype for interviews, with pre-scheduled discussion times, can help alleviate this issue. For example, we conduct many interviews with very senior people such as physicians, heads of science, managing directors and senior procurement professionals in the NHS, as well as industry experts and other customers. They do not have much time, but many are surprisingly willing to commit, especially if an incentive is involved.
Covering sensitive issues	Nearly always conduct them one-to-one, so the respondent is less inhibited. Use projective techniques and sensitive questioning and probing to get under the skin. Customers open up in a way that is just not possible within a stable supplier/buyer relationship.

More complicated issues	It is important to be well acquainted with the subject matter. People conducting the interviews will need to rapidly get to grips with the terminology and market situation, its players and issues.
Cannot get six people to group discussions	Experience tells us that in B2B, face-to-face-depth interviews work better, are more effective, fit more with the customer's timetable and result in more truthful answers.
Feedback required	In B2B research, some people may ask for feedback. This needs to be handled sensitively and should be very bland in nature, but it must be recognisable as the truth. If people have asked for it, then it must be given.
Talking to your customers in this way is a positive communication medium	In every B2B project we have been involved in, the customers have not only welcomed the initiative of our clients, but it is often the first time they have ever been asked to help.
In B2B, online is as powerful a research tool as it is in B2C	Studying the data around how your customers are interacting with your digital platforms throughout the buying process is a rich vein of data, ready to be turned into useful insight.
Don't forget your customers' customers	Helping your customer understand its customers helps build relationships and competitive advantage.

To know your starting place, you will still need to work out levels of awareness and understanding of your company within the minds of customers. You can construct an Experience Audit, which examines the current omnichannel CX using the framework of control, access, fit, sense, continuity and flow. You will need to go to the frontline and to the senior teams to establish the ambition for the company and explore the hunches and ideas from within. To get a picture of the future and avoid being trapped in the 'here and now', you must go to the 'jungle' and explore a little differently, and, of course, you will need to 'prove it with data' and link insight to business benefit wherever you can.

2. Visioning

There is very little difference in the need or the method to create a vision within B2B when compared to B2C. A clearly articulated vision, robustly researched, can transform a business just as much as it can in B2C. The B2B company uses the Exploring output to develop a vision through a collaborative, interactive workshop and then tests it internally and, where it can, externally. Once again, there is no room for jargon, the objectives need to be focused, and clear judgement criteria need to be established.

Don't make it personal

Sometimes it is more difficult to get a senior team to accept where they sit in a market – in B2B, it can sometimes feel more personal. One professional services company simply could not accept that its customers regarded its sector as having commodified itself, and there was no difference in the customer's mind between one supplier and another. Indeed, the differentiation was so limited, their customers ran panels of suppliers to spread the risk. All the highly professional skills they offered, and the qualifications for which they had studied for many years to obtain, were not points of competitive advantage. What they had not seen was the differentiating power of the data they collected and the client need to understand it and gain advantage from the insights and operational efficiencies it could bring.

The B2B difference	What to do about it
The vision needs to speak to the business and take into account the complexity of the relationships	There is no room for flowery concepts or fluffy thinking here: B2B relationships are more personal than B2C. The need to recognise the brand as a business tool to drive business behaviours and success is essential.
Numbers, numbers, numbers	If the brand vision cannot be directly related to business data, and especially the KPIs, used by the senior management team to run the business or customer relationships, then it is back to square one.
Win over the sceptics in complex multi-functional teams	Getting the right people on the bus is critical to success, and getting them to buy in to the brand vision is a must-have for success. There is no better way than showing these people the financial and quantifiable opportunities.

Choose your consultants carefully	The irony doesn't escape us! Finding the right people to support the team – who have the same passion about your business, who invest time in getting to know what you do, why you do it, how you do it and to what end – usually wins over even the most hard-nosed cynic.
Always go back to the evidence	The strongest argument for change is the pressure for change itself. If you believe what your customers are telling you, then you are half way to developing the right brand vision. If you don't, then a state of hubris is only just around the corner, with all the negative outcomes that can deliver.
Keep looking outside rather than inside	If you organise your business in such a way that it's easy for the business to manage itself, then prepare for a lot of free time! In B2B, the development of passionate and aligned relationships that are guided by a brand vision that inspires your own people and customers is a priority.

Make sure the people who own the customer relationships are inspired by your vision	In B2B we have fewer customers, and each tends to be worth more individually to us than B2C – we should know, as we are a B2B business. If your customer-facing teams are not inspired by the vision, then you need to go back to the drawing board. Without these people, it's going to be very difficult to deliver what you want.
Great vision attracts the best talent	Good people want to work for winning teams with a clear sense of direction, opportunities to grow and challenges to stretch them. The vision is what turns them on and excites them.

3. Aligning

Creating the envisioned CX that aligns to the brand is critical in the B2B environment. Businesses are incredibly critical of other businesses that try to sell to them, who say one thing about themselves and then deliver something completely different. Alignment is key. You have to do what you say you will, or you will be dropped like a stone. To create Hot CX in B2B, it needs to be envisioned from an omnichannel perspective, the jobs and objectives of clients must provide the framework for delivery, and the basics and amplifiers need to be identified. They will be different to the ones that drive B2C CX, but they are important nevertheless and they need to be tested.

Balls

We were recently asked to sit in on a big pitch presentation for a major national retailer's social media business, where we experienced a very tense moment. The pitcher started talking through their brand values with his prospective client and focused on the fantastic 'always on' attitude they had to client service. He then nonchalantly revealed a list of great service elements that they offer, including a commitment to always answering the phone inside three rings. As you might expect, the client asked him to prove it. The pitcher nervously glanced around the room, put the phone on speaker, drew breath and called.

Ring, ring…

Ring, ring…

Hello, you are through to Blaggins and Bloggins; my name is Hazel, how can I help you?

Phew.

Brows were wiped and the pitcher's breathing restarted.

And they won.

The B2B difference	What to do about it
B2B customer journeys tend to be longer and more complex	Envisioning the B2B customer journey is a complex job, but it follows the same basic principles as any B2C mapping exercise: the executional difference is in the understanding of complexity and time.
You don't get anywhere without a business case	While this is a similar point to B2C, we have always felt it comes up as an objective much more clearly in B2B, and the data is often more available and therefore helps drive cause and effect through root-cause analysis.
The scale means there are more decision makers and potential gatekeepers	There are multiple influencers in the customer journey. Each needs to be engaged on the journey and the brand needs to deliver a solution at each touchpoint. It's a complex balancing act, but very rewarding when you get it right.

B2B teams are complex and have multiple skills and capabilities that need to be in tune and ready to support	Making sure the whole chain of influence is engaged in envisioning the customer experience is important for the business and the team. This process brings them together, often for the first time, to map how your business will be managing its relationships with customers. Having the team together will save conflict, duplication and inefficiency in the future.
Customer-journey mapping can be personalised to a much greater extent	Unlike B2C, any B2B customer journey can be individualised and personalised to meet the specific needs of a single customer in order to answer their specific needs.
Expertise must be applied	Your customers come to you for your expertise in the services and products you supply. This must always be visible to them at each and every interaction throughout the customer journey.
Knowing what the customer needs to achieve from the relationship is critical	We should know this, given the evidence from the Exploring stage, but we need to make sure the brand nails this at each touchpoint to build the delivered relationship.

Identifying the brand basics for your sector allows your brand to do them better than anyone else	In most B2B environments, getting the basics right is a no brainer, although often overlooked by some in the market. Getting them right and using the brand to improve them can help to differentiate a unique approach and style that only you can deliver.
Amplifying your brand will be less about recommending a friend and more about nail this and the next deal	In B2C we use Brand Amplification to drive social media noise, as consumers become part of the media and communications effort. In B2B, recommending a friend isn't a main driver, but nailing the next deal is. Brand Amplification in B2B is designed to boost the specialness of the relationship and the potential to enhance the longer-term relationship.
Rigour and diligent delivery are second nature in B2B	It's vital to have a well-mapped customer journey that identifies every touch point, what the brand will deliver at each and how we want customers to feel.

4. Delivering

"You are defined by what you do, not what you say you are going to do"
CARL JUNG

If it was critical in B2C, it is utterly essential in B2B. Unfulfilled promises will mean the end of any business relationship, regardless of friendship and the personal bonds involved in many business-to-business relationships. Delivering Hot CX in B2B means that the right people need to be on the Delivering bus, the picture must be kept in sight, silos need to be busted and a blueprint for delivery is required to guide the process. As with B2C, early wins are needed, and pilots can really help and take some of the risk out of any change involved when the stakes are high.

Making it hard for themselves

As if the complex world of supporting drug companies with compliance consulting weren't enough, one of our clients wanted to merge its consultancy services with a business-process outsourcing company to form an end-to-end delivery approach for the global pharmaceutical market. This meant different geographies, cultures and client understanding.

The rigorous approach adopted from Exploring, Visioning and Aligning was all well and good, but they had to deliver. Exploring had given us clear evidence that, while the strategy was interesting and something customers wanted, there was a scepticism about whether it could be pulled off. The global nature of the new business, with centres in each continent, required a delivery plan that was driven by the vision and matched the alignment strategy, with plans for each department that had been developed by a multifunctional team.

The main board drove the plan and each department had advocates who kept the plan on track.

The company is now answering more RFPs than ever, and has quickly become recognised for its specialist expertise and ability to meet the needs as a major brand in its market, that delivers what it says it is going to deliver.

The B2B difference	What to do about it
The devil will always be in the detail and its depth	Delivering a B2B customer experience will require customer experiences that can be both high level and granular, often at the same touchpoint.
The buying system that drives the customer experience will be iterative and lengthy	Unlike B2C customer experiences in the B2B space, we need to build in the iterations as a natural part of the experience, each one offering an opportunity to build (or destroy) the brand.
It will always be their timetable and not yours	In B2C, the final collision with a consumer and a sale tends to be at point of purchase, be that on or offline. With B2B we see a much lengthier process driven by the needs of the customer, so your CX must work within the grain of their business and not just your own.

Delivering your CX must focus on building closer relationships with your customers	B2B customers want more in the way of closer relationships, to enable them to gain information and support throughout their experience with the brand. They tend to seek more depth in the experience to help them achieve what they are looking to do.
The B2B customer knows their stuff; helping them build their knowledge helps deliver competitive advantage	Unlike the B2C customer, those in the B2B world tend to have encyclopaedic knowledge of their business, sector and competitive offers. Delivering any CX in this environment must enable the team to match and build on this customer knowledge with insights that differentiate and make the competition look less informed and less expert.
Keeping the brand at the core of the CX is essential to delivering a consistency that customers seek	In B2B, risk reduction is a vital customer need, and so your CX must provide the rigour in delivery that enables customers to see and feel the brand. The reassurance of a consistent brand, delivered by inspiring people who want both you and them to win, is what we are all looking for.
Make things happen quickly, pilot and improve in order to show the business the value of the process	We don't know of one B2B relationship that is not seeking to maintain the status quo. We are all changing, iterating, sprinting and scrumming to stay ahead. Making it happen is brand critical.

5. Measuring

The metrics may be different to B2C, but measurement is still crucial. The mantra of 'if it doesn't get measured, it doesn't get done' may not be quite right, but it sure has a big influence when you measure something and your colleagues know who is responsible for which numbers. You will need a baseline read of the start situation, work out what CX data impacts the business most, and track changes using both hard and soft data. If you have one metric to do it all with, success, though not assured, is very much more likely.

The B2B difference	What to do about it
Data and insights into your customers' customers is critical to building depth into your relationship	You should try to know as much about the needs of your client's customers as you do about your client's needs – after all, you are an integral part of customer delivery to their customers. Knowing what the end user will want in the future helps you innovate and advise your customers, and often helps protect margins.
Understanding their data and customer measures helps build closer relationships	Building business cases around the whole Brand Alignment approach will prove the return that can be delivered to the business.
Openness with data builds trust and deepens relationships	Being able to build insights from the data-gathering process and relating that back to your brand and its abilities to perform for customers keeps the rigour and discipline centre stage.

Use data to drive rapid change	We live in a world of rapid prototyping and 'doing it yesterday', so we must use our data to continuously improve what we are doing and iterate our customer experience in order to enhance the value we deliver to them.
Your measurement of experience must match their measurement of business performance	Aligning your key-satisfaction measures to business outcomes for the customer is critical in the B2B environment: it illustrates the interconnectivity of the two organisations and can drive open behaviours on both sides.

B2B: what's hot and what's not

Hot	Not
Supporting your team with deep insights from data and analytics	Keeping your data too close to your chest
Really understanding what the customer is trying to achieve through a relationship with you	Fitting them into your standard operating model
Looking at the customer journey as omnichannel and driven by the customer's behaviours	Seeing it as a digital and then physical experience
Knowing your customer's customers well enough to help them improve their relationship with those customers	Just looking at what you do as an input to your customer's processes

Inspiring your customer-facing teams with great vision	Thinking of them only as employees
Creating a place where the best people want to work	Just making up the numbers for the service-level agreement (SLA)
Constantly iterating and improving the way you work with your customers	Sticking to rigid and inflexible SLAs that don't mean anything
Building a bespoke customer journey for each customer	Operating a one-size-fits-all approach
Delivering the granularity with as much energy as the strategic pitch	Forgetting that the devil is in the detail
Keeping your performance measurement and analysis as a dashboard the two organisations can use	Keeping your data to yourself and trying to keep your customers in the dark

CONCLUSION

So you think you want a revolution?

Remember the slide we wrote in 2000, only to see it again in a keynote speech at a conference in 2015?

The first era of branding was that a brand is what it says it is.
The second era of branding is that a brand is what it does. We are in
the era of experience branding.

It was presented to herald the start of a revolution – a consumer revolution where a brand's success is determined by the multi-channel, or omnichannel, experience it delivers. Advertising was deemed as 'still important' in shaping a company's future, but has been relegated in the hierarchy of influence.

The truth is that the consumer revolution isn't coming – it isn't even here. It has been and gone. The revolution from the consumer perspective has already happened, and the new era is well and truly established and is not going away. Consumers have been far ahead of business on this one, leaving companies and organisations adapting and trying to align around a new set of consumer rules. There are many reasons for this slowness to adapt: many companies do not have customer experience as part of their culture, short-term objectives get in the way, legacy systems, silos and no link to KPIs have all stood in the way, the effects of which have been well documented.

Another reason it took so long for business to realise it had to change is the vested interest of agencies and the reluctance of marketers to accept it. They are the ones who probably knew the revolution was coming first, but they didn't want to admit it. Let's face it: it's more difficult building brands this way – new skills and techniques will need to be learned and, on the surface anyway, it's not as much fun.

The great news is that we now have a new generation of marketers and many of them can see that the new era is probably the best thing that ever happened to their discipline. Because the whole company is responsible for the customer experience, the brand is now a company-wide responsibility. This means they will always be on the bus and now they can get nearer the driving seat, as the discipline should be at the forefront of the change that is happening. It is also becoming clear that the skills and techniques required are exciting and that it is much more fun than they originally thought, partly because it is real, partly because it involves people at every stage, and partly because it has exciting innovation and customers at its heart.

Business is now beginning to view the CX and branding as one and the same. We have many friends who now have 'customer experience' and 'brand' in their title, which is a sure-fire way of recognising that the world is changing fast. This should be rejoiced, as CX was nearly hijacked by the digitisers. At the start of the revolution, customer experience was often put into the digital or user-experience category, as it was easier to silo it away and the shiny new toys and the clever new apps of that world were much sexier than the old-fashioned physical touchpoints that used to dominate.

The digital emphasis, of course, is understandable. The digital revolution has improved customer experience by a previously unimaginable degree, and now sets expectations for experiences in the physical world. Customers can access more information, and more instantly, about what they are buying and where they are buying from, they can order from their front room, interact at will, share their experience and have more fun than ever before. The pre-digital CX bears no comparisons to the post-digital one – it is so much better now. But, to ignore the fact that people generally mesh their interactions – so that they dance between digital (search online, look at reviews) to physical (pop into the shop, browse, chat to staff) to digital (buy online) and back to physical again (delivery to home) – would be dangerous, as it is simply not real. The customer experience is made up of interactions across all the channels. It is delivered by people in stores, on telephones, in vans, through apps, websites, social media, on television, posters and newspapers. Or, in one word, omnichannel.

We could see this coming back in 2000. We didn't really know how to prepare for the revolution and spent the first eight years trying to find out what was happening and what skills we would need. As soon as we thought we had it sussed, the market would move on and we would be left, stranded, to dust ourselves off. We didn't have to start all over again, but we did have to reappraise and work out what to do next.

But we did put our money where our mouths are, and we 'came out' in 2000 and pronounced that advertising was dead and 'long live brand-driven omnichannel customer experience'. It was a bit bold, and we were rightly given a tough time by some of our ex-peers (in a friendly way, of course). Looking back to those times, one of the things that didn't help was that there was no acceptable lexicon of CX. Nobody mentioned CX or UX, and omnichannel didn't exist, so we weren't really able to say 'long live brand-driven omnichannel customer experience'. In fact, we had no words for it at all for a couple of years, until we came up with 'brand alignment' and talked about 'aligning through the whole experience'. Yet the remarkable similarity between our 2000 slide (which we wrote for our first-ever pitch, by the way) and the one we saw in 2015 surely proves that we meant the same thing. The result is that the fog has now cleared and most people can see what has happened. Anyone looking at building a brand-led, compelling customer experience today will need a whole set of specialist skills, some of which they didn't know existed 10 years ago. This includes market researchers, innovators, process-change specialists, business analysts, customer-journey mappers, experience designers, brand strategists and, of course, UX designers and technologists. An eclectic mix, but what a great mix – what a great new world it is.

However, this great new world has its challenges. The stakes are getting higher and there is competition at every turn. New companies with global reach are springing up in places that we would never have considered in the old era: people's front rooms, isolated parts of Cornwall and in some far-flung parts of Asia. Add to this that people, as we have heard earlier, will compare your experience to others from outside your sector, and the feeling is that the battle to succeed and to put dinner on your plate is becoming more and more intense, meaning you can never become complacent. Furthermore, building and delivering compelling customer experience is not a one-off event: it is a continuum, an ever-evolving and improving process that must be able to respond to changes in environment, competition, disruption and, of course, customer behaviours.

'Every morning in Africa, a gazelle wakes up. It knows it must run faster than the fastest lion or it will be killed. Every morning, a lion wakes up. It knows it must outrun the slowest gazelle or it will starve to death. It doesn't matter whether you are a lion or a gazelle: when the sun comes up, you'd better be running.'
African proverb

We recently chaired a CX conference where we met the Director of Future Payments at a global bank. He told us a story where developments in touch-payment technology have opened up a whole new market for them.

Previously, they had not targeted teenage girls, but now, with the sale of embedded technology in accessories, these girls can charge a bangle up with money and use it to go shopping. How cool is that? (Although I will give it a miss personally.) All this has been brought about by new collaborations between the bank and the new wave of solution providers.

It is amazing to think that less than 10 years ago, a stranger in your house was most likely a burglar – now, they are more than likely an Airbnb guest. These digitally-powered businesses really took off with the launch of the Apple iPhone back in 2007, when smartphones became more accessible to the masses than ever before. This mobile revolution and the disruptive CX movement have caused many so-called legacy businesses and brands to panic about the impact they are having. However, we still have hotels, bed and breakfasts and taxis – and a few bookshops, for that matter.

We should think a bit differently about the 'disruptors', as they are doing every brand a favour. Their challenge to the legacy brands is to force them to up their game and deliver experiences that customers want, in ways that customers want. They have raised the benchmark of experience expectation higher and more rapidly than many can cope with using older business models. The most significant aspect of all this is that they have done it through Delivery – it works brilliantly when you interact with it and the brand is built through the power of customer amplification through its social networks. Long gone are the days when you told six friends about a good or bad experience – now, you measure the level of sharing in millions.

While much time, energy and money is being spent on developing the most effective UX and most helpful data-analysis combos, there is a danger that all this might do is create another corporate silo – the digital silo. Many people are happily bashing away at code and algorithms to develop amazingly seamless and friction-free digital experiences that all fall over when the customer interacts with the physical brand – which, in most markets, they have to, and indeed often want to, at some stage of the experience.

As we heard in the Aligning chapter, the UX versus CX debate isn't really a debate. While businesses often silo digital and the physical delivery departments in order to organise themselves in a traditional way that is the most convenient for themselves, the customer doesn't see the difference. They just see the total experience, for better or for worse. To them, it is one brand delivering one experience.

Customers see a brand and an experience that naturally communicates how it feels about them through everything it does, regardless of whether it is digital or physical. It could be dirty loos, queues, grumpy telephone responses, ill-informed customer-service people, waiting times on phones, a 'you're wrong' attitude, apps that crash, clunky web design, inflexible delivery and so on, but the brutal truth is that every one of these experiences is a point of communication far more powerful than any advertising campaign.

So the answer, in a nutshell, is to use the brand to drive a compelling omnichannel customer experience. The danger with all this is that improvement, important though it is, becomes the be-all and end-all of omnichannel CX change, and we all end up back where many of us started, with no differentiation or competitive advantage.

The beauty of CX development, using the brand in an inclusive and collaborative way, is that the process itself has a transformational effect and the customer really benefits, if it's done well.

- It creates an experience that makes customers feel the brand understands them and is with them.
- The customer feels they are engaging with one brand across every channel, and delivery will be consistent: same positioning, values and personality throughout.
- The people they encounter on their journey to transaction are brand builders, delivering a positive human face to the brand.

191

- It is the proof that the business is serious about its people and customers.

To deliver the CX in this way will require a change in approach. No longer can everyone devolve responsibility for the brand and its customers to the marketing department alone. This responsibility now resides across the whole organisation, and, as a result, silos must be busted and people need to understand customers and the vision for their brand and where they fit in to its delivery. Change has to happen. With competition as it is, there is no other option, and we have outlined some top tips and a process through which to do it.

The first thing to remember is that you don't have to do everything at once. You can chunk it up and prioritise wherever you can in alignment with what you already have: the business needs, capability and goals, and you can always hold off completing some of the work until you start seeing returns on your investment. Like the Realist says, you can't eat an elephant in one sitting.

But somewhere along the line, you need to be pretty sure you have the customer and the business at the heart of everything, so you need to go Exploring; you will need an inspiring and differentiating vision for the brand, a developed and aligned omnichannel CX and a plan to deliver and measure progress.

Exploring must start internally, at the top. You will need an understanding of the business vision, the timescales, how the organisation works, and you need to be aware of the appetite and capability for change. You also need to mesh hard-data analysis and softer customer research to get real, robust omnichannel insight and have a view of the future so that you don't base everything on the here and now.

The vision for the brand will need to be based on the Exploring output, constructed collaboratively and be simply expressed (remember, we all need to get it), deliverable and tested qualitatively and quantitatively. The vision for the omnichannel CX must align to the brand vision, be customer centric, constructed collaboratively and brought to life through film so that people can see what the end game is and be inspired to deliver it.

Next, you need to add the detail around the envisioned omnichannel CX. It will pinpoint the basics of delivery and you will need specialist innovation skills to develop brand amplifiers. The change in the CX will have multi-channel implications, and it needs to be tested with customers, potential customers and colleagues and then captured in a high-level illustration so that everyone can see the big picture and understand where they fit in.

Delivering is where it all comes together, and you start to see the fruits of your labour. You need the right people on the bus, and a Delivery Blueprint – and make sure you have some quick wins, pilots in place and that you keep the big picture and business reality in mind at all times.

Measuring is the final piece in the jigsaw. Some people say that nothing gets done without this. It needs a combination of the business data you probably already have and customer measurements taken across the whole CX.

Put this all together and you will achieve 'Hot CX', Customer Experience for Realists. It is not just improvement, it is brand-led customer experience that is compelling and leads to business success in the real world. When we came out back in 2000, we could see that the consumer world was changing but had no idea how to respond to it, and we meandered around, trying all sorts of things to make it work. The joy is that now we are not alone; nobody disputes its leading role in business and nobody questions anymore why we left JWT. Coming out was tricky at the time, but now everyone is doing it.

A footnote

I recently went through the process of buying a new car (not my favourite experience). At one showroom, Mercedes-Benz, I soon realised that I was about to encounter a new type of experience.

The man who greeted me proudly proclaimed that he was a 'product expert' – note, not a 'salesman' – and that he would answer any questions I had about the various cars I was looking at. This, he said, 'kept the process more friendly and less salesy'. He was obviously very proud of the new process and very good at answering all my questions. He then sat me down and revealed his trump card: a marvellous app that helped me work out the essentials, the nice to haves and the definitely to be avoided (the only thing I put in this column was the colour white). I then proceeded to build my very own, personalised car. Oh, yes! It was a brilliant experience: I could add things, take them out, change the colour and see what the car looked like on screen. Having concluded the 'fantasy-car-building stage', as I liked to call it, he then left me and in moved the salesman.

He was equally charming, not at all salesy, so it was clear they had been through some kind of CX/UX development revolution, and it wasn't his fault when it all fell down. The weird car that I had just created simply didn't exist, and when we added up the cost of all the bits and pieces I wanted, the car was way above what I was prepared to pay. It all fell down because, although the CX and UX were well aligned, the customer was not central to the process, and the sheer practical issues of people like me creating a Frankenstein car that doesn't exist just hadn't been accounted for. This all goes to show how difficult it is.

The end to this story... I bought a Škoda.

Hot CX: what's hot and what's not

Hot	Not
Using the brand to drive a compelling customer experience that drives business success	Improving alone
Omnichannel	Being channel-biased
Balancing the needs of the customer with those of the business	Improving for improvement's sake
Silo-bustin' engagement	Wall building
Basing decisions on brutal truths and robust data	A finger-in-the-air approach
Fast, agile and continuously improving. Digital speed in a physical environment	Being static and staid
Focusing on how the brand wants customers to feel	Basing improvements on maximising internal efficiencies

Resourcing efficiently, as it stops you doing the things you don't need to do	Not having a lens to aid decision-making
Branding the key category basics and amplifying where it matters	Disrespecting the basics and not standing out
Focusing on the now, but with a view to the horizon	Being too focused on the here and now

REFERENCES

Anderton, E. and Bevan, S. (2014). Constrained Work? Job Enrichment & Employee Engagement In Low Wage, Low Skill Jobs. The Work Foundation. (Source: http://www.theworkfoundation.com/wp-content/uploads/2017/07/350_Constrained-Work-Final.pdf)

Aon Hewitt, (2011), Trends in Global Employee Engagement. (Source: http://www.aon.com/attachments/thought-leadership/Trends_Global_Employee_Engagement_Final.pdf)

Aon Hewitt, (2012). Global employee engagement database. London: Aon Hewitt.

Bain & Company, (2015), Closing the delivery gap, (Source: http://bain.com/bainweb/pdfs/cms/hotTopics/closingdeliverygap.pdf

Collins, J., (2001), Good to Great, Random House Business.

Crandell, C,.Forbes, (2013), Customer Experience: Is It the Chicken or Egg? (Source: https://www.forbes.com/sites/christinecrandell/2013/01/21/customer-experience-is-it-the-chicken-or-egg/#138fa2293557)

D'Emidio, T., Dorton, D. and Duncan, E., (2015), Service innovation in a digital world, McKinsey (Source: https://www.mckinsey.com/business-functions/operations/our-insights/service-innovation-in-a-digital-world)

Doughty, S., (2011), 'Sir Fred's Affair: Why We Do Have A Right To

REFERENCES

Know', The Daily Mail, May 20.

Engagement through the brand has operational and financial benefit, Kenexa 2011, Towers Watson 2012, Aon Hewitt 2010, CBI

Flade, P., (2003), Great Britain's Workforce Lacks Inspiration. Gallup. (Source: http://news.gallup.com/businessjournal/9847/great-britains-workforce-lacks-inspiration.aspx)

Gartner, (2015), Gartner Predicts a Customer Experience Battlefield, Contributor: Tom McCall

Gartner, (2015), Customer Experience Metrics Evolve Beyond Net Promoter Score, Contributor: Levy, H. P., (Source: https://www.gartner.com/smarterwithgartner/customer-experience-metrics-evolve-beyond-net-promoter-score/)

Gibb, F., Savage, M., Griffiths, K., (2011), 'Sir Fred exposed as injunction breached', The Times, May 20.

Harvard Business Review, 2015, comparison of aligned and non-aligned businesses

Hawke, S., (2011), 'Fred The Bed! Ex-RBS chief had affair with employee'. The Sun, May 20.

Magids, S., Zorfas, A. and Leeman, D., (2015). The New Science of Customer Emotions, Harvard Business Review (Source: https://hbr.org/2015/11/the-new-science-of-customer-emotions)

Marshall, J., Cunningham. T. and Rosenburg, E., (2013), The Secret Sauce Of Top Companies: Aligning Your Consumer Brand And Your Talent Brand, Lippincott. (Source: https://business.linkedin.com/content/dam/business/talent-solutions/regional/APAC/Perspective_Align_Your_Consumer_and_Talent_Brand_LinkedIn.pdf)

mcorp.cx, (n.d), Getting Your Customer Experience to Deliver on Your Brand Promise: An Action List. (Source: https://www.mcorpcx.com/articles/getting-customer-experience-deliver-brand-promise-action-list)

Murphy, E. and Murphy M. (2002) Leading on the Edge of Chaos. Prentice Hall

Reichheld, F., (2003), One Number You Need to Grow, Harvard Business Review, (Source: https://hbr.org/2003/12/the-one-number-you-need-to-grow)

Right Management (2006), Measuring True Employee Engagement, Right Management

Robison, J., (2010), M&A the Right Way. Gallup, (Source: http://news.gallup.com/businessjournal/142859/right.aspx)

Sorenson, S., (2013), How Employee Engagement Drives Growth, Gallup, (Source: http://news.gallup.com/businessjournal/163130/employee-engagement-drives-growth.aspx)

Stable, D., (2015), Measuring Customer Experience: Key Performance Indicators for Customer Communications Management, Documentmedia.com, (Source: http://documentmedia.com/article-1970-Measuring-Customer-Experience-Key-Performance-Indicators-for-Customer-Communications-Management.html)

Throton, K., (2013), SalesForce (blog) 18 Interesting Stats to Get You Rethinking Your Customer Service Process. (Source: https://www.salesforce.com/blog/2013/08/customer-service-stats.html)

Towers Watson, (2012) Global Workforce Study: Engagement at Risk: Driving Strong Performance in a Volatile Global Environment. (Source: https://www.towerswatson.com/en-GB/Insights/IC-Types/Survey-Research-Results/2012/07/2012-Towers-Watson-Global-Workforce-Study)

Walker, (2013), Customers 2020: A Progress Report. (Source: https://www.walkerinfo.com/customers2020/)

Yohn, D., (2016), Design Your Employee Experience as Thoughtfully as You Design Your Customer Experience. Harvard Business Review. (Source: https://hbr.org/2016/12/design-your-employee-experience-as-thoughtfully-as-you-design-your-customer-experience)

ABOUT THE AUTHORS

Gary Moss, aka Moose
Email: gary.moss@brand-vista.com

Gary began his career as a Market Analyst with Thorn EMI in 1986 before joining J Walter Thompson as a Junior Brand Planner in 1989. There, he enjoyed working with a range of companies such as Boots, Esso and The Tussauds Group. Gary became Strategy Director and Managing Director of JWT in 1996 but soon left to found Brand Vista in 2000 where he works with companies such as Merlin Entertainments (which operates brands including Madame Tussauds, SEA LIFE, The London Eye, LEGOLAND and Alton Towers), ODEON, ASDA, Vision Express, Astra Zeneca, The Jockey Club, PREZZO, Mitchells and Butlers, The Times Newspaper, David Lloyd, MBNA, Betfred and Gala Bingo. He currently puts all his extra career-related energy into his role as a trustee at The National Space Centre and speaks regularly at industry events.

Andrew Stothert, aka Stoat
Email: andrew.stothert@brand-vista.com

Andrew began his career in the early 1980s, working for his father to sell soft drinks from the back of lorries and before long, he was running the Barrs Irn-Bru and Tizer brands. Some years later, Andrew moved to JWT, London where he worked with brands including Rowntree and Golden Wonder. Five years later, he moved back to Barrs as Group Marketing Manager and a few years after that, Andrew was headhunted back to JWT, Manchester where he first met Gary. It was here that Andrew worked as CEO for six years before leaving to found Brand Vista in 2000.

Andrew continues to work across many of Brand Vista's client portfolio, as well as developing new solutions to clients' challenges and needs, and speaking regularly at CX conferences.

* * * * *

Thank you for reading.

Gary and Andrew are the co-founders of Brand Vista,
a Customer Experience consultancy, which helps the
world's leading brands develop irresistible customer
experiences.

If you want to contact either Gary or Andrew, or find out
more about Brand Vista and Hot CX, visit our website:

brand-vista.com

Printed in Poland
by Amazon Fulfillment
Poland Sp. z o.o., Wrocław